Athlete

_____

Season

_____

Team/Club

_____

The Athlete's Workbook

A Season of Sport and Reflection

Richard Kent, PhD

A companion book to

Writing on the Bus: Using Athletic Team Notebooks and Journals to Advance Learning and Performance in Sports

For my writing coaches... Michael Armstrong, James Britton, Jared Carter, Dixie Goswami, Harvey Kail, Thomas Newkirk, Catherine Puiia, Gayle Sirois, Anne Wood, and JoAnne Zywna... *and my athletes.*

Acknowledgements... Thanks to those who provided feedback along the way: Amy Edwards, Gonzaga University; Nicole Moore, Stetson University; Jason B. Jones, Las Vegas; Ken Martin, University of Maine; Sheila Stawinski, University of Vermont; and Chris Nightingale, University of Maine.

NATIONAL WRITING PROJECT

This book is published in cooperation with the National Writing Project, University of California, 2105 Bancroft Way, Berkeley, CA 94720

Contents

"To get to the finish line, you'll have to try lots of different paths."

–Amby Burfoot
Boston Marathon Winner, 1968

Introduction

The workbook you have in your hands can help you to become a better athlete. By completing the book's activities, you will stay more organized and learn more about your sport and about yourself as a competitor. This is exactly what many world-class athletes do to move to the next level.

This workbook will not replace good coaching or dedicated training. You're not going to instantaneously run faster or score more goals because you wrote reflections about your training or kept a log. But maintaining this workbook will make you a more knowledgeable athlete, and with that knowledge you will improve.

The Basics

Depending on how often you train or choose to write, this workbook can accommodate a sports season of 2 ½ to 6 months. Along with 72 Training Logs and Athletic Writing Prompts, you will find a wide variety of other helpful activities. Here are a few suggestions about keeping this workbook:

- *Just Write It.* Don't be overly concerned with perfect writing. In other words, don't stop to check spelling, correct grammar, or create perfect paragraphs.

- *Quick Write:* When you're responding to the prompts try a Quick Write: write nonstop for 3 to 6 minutes. Do not take your pen or pencil off the paper. Just keep writing. If your mind goes blank, make a list of words related to the topic until you start writing sentences again. Here's an example of a Quick Write by a tennis player who lost to a less-skilled player. Notice the list of words in the middle:

> *I don't like losing to someone I should have beaten. At first, it*
> *feels like a bad dream. I think about some of the points I messed*

up and should have won. I think about... double faults, over swinging, loss of control, emotions, anger, lack of focus... I know I can prevent most of my double faults. They usually happen because I get too emotional and I lose focus. I have to stay in control of my emotions and stay in the moment. THAT'S IT! Staying in the moment. Staying in the moment. I let my mind go back to a mistake when what I really need to do is stay focused on the point I'm playing....

- *Word Web.* If you struggle to write one of the prompts in this workbook, try making a Word Web. Check out the example in Figure 1. Place the athletic writing prompts in the middle of the page and then list words that connect to the topic. Once you have 8-10 words, start writing about each word. You'll be surprised how your thoughts flow.

- *Draw or sketch.* There are many ways to tell the story of your training and competing. Even if you can barely sketch stick figures, give drawing a try.

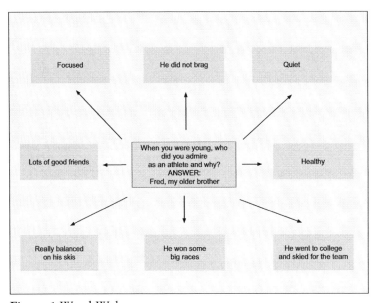

Figure 1 Word Web

- *Switch Prompts.* If you have a burning issue that needs addressing, save the day's journal prompt for another time and write about what's important to you. If one of the prompts doesn't work for you, turn to the back of your workbook and select one from the additional 50 Athletic Writing Prompts.

- *When should you write?* Some athletes find it helpful to write the journals at the same time each day, like after a training session or before bedtime. Do what works best for you. The Training Logs and the Competition Analysis pages should be filled out after a workout or competition so the performance is fresh in your mind.

- Protect Your Workbook. Many athletes keep their workbooks in a zip-lock plastic bag in their gym bags.

Training Log

A Training Log is a place for you to record your workouts. Adapt this log in ways that work best for you. Several times during the season, you'll be prompted to go back and review your log. Such reflection will keep you informed and help you revise your training when necessary.

The building blocks of effective training like proper sleep impact your health and sports performance. Each day you'll be asked to give a quick snapshot of yourself as an athlete:

Hours of sleep: *9*   Body weight: *145*   Health: O   Hydration: +
(+) Above Average, (O) Average, and (–) Below Average

The nutrition checklist serves as a reminder that eating properly is a necessity for the serious athlete. List how many servings you've eaten of these basic food groups. And remember: you can get much more information on nutrition from your coach, trainer, and sports nutrition books.

Nutrition: *5 Grains*   *2 Veggies*   *3 Fruits*   *3 Protein*

Keeping track of sleep, hydration, weight, and general health can help you and your coach identify the causes of performance issues that may surface. Let's say you start to drag at practice because you lack energy. Check the previous 5-7 days in your log. How many below average (–) health days have you marked? Are you getting enough sleep? Enough water? Your logs may tell you to get to bed earlier or to start carrying a water bottle with you to improve hydration. Olympic Gold Medalist Joan Benoit Samuelson said, "Your body will tell you what to do." Listen... and read back through your workbook.

The chart in Figure 2 will help you identify your Training Intensity Level. Too much high intensity work can cause fatigue and overtraining. The Training Plan you or your coach developed may have 5 or 6 intensity levels or none at all. In the case of more levels, just adapt your log. If recording Intensity Levels hasn't been a part of your plan before, start now. These levels can provide a more complete picture of your training.

Training Intensity Level	Training Type	Breathing/Pace
1	Recovery level, Relaxed and comfortable training	Slow pace Very easy to talk
2	Low to medium intensity, Easy aerobic	Medium pace Easy to talk
3	High intensity, sustained training; Threshold training	Race pace Difficult to talk

Figure 2 Training Intensity Level

Adapt your Training Log to fit your sport and you. For example, if you play basketball, you may wish to record the number of foul shots you take each day. Figure 3 shows an example of a baseball infielder's Training Log during preseason. Notice the rectangle on the bottom left of the figure. This space is provided so you can capture that day's training with (+) Above Average, (O) Average, and (–) Below Average. This snapshot of your training will be helpful as the season progresses.

Competition Analysis I & II

Near the end of the workbook, you'll find 25 copies of the Competition Analysis I and a model. You may not have 25 "official" competitions in your sports season; however, the forms may be used for scrimmages, *friendlies*, or intrasquad contests. The prompts on these sheets will help you analyze one of your competitions. You may have to adapt some questions, depending on your sport. For example, if you golf as an individual in tournaments, *Team Weakness* may not apply.

Three times during your sports season, you'll be given an opportunity to analyze a competition that you've watched in person, on TV, or online. The Competition Analysis II can help you look more objectively at the games or competitions you watch. The CAII is a learning tool that will challenge you to watch a competition more critically, more fully, and more like a coach than an athlete. Developing a "coach's eye" as an athlete is next level learning in sports.

Injury Rehabilitation Plan

This form will help you stay organized with your rehabilitation program after an injury. It's best if you fill out the Injury Rehabilitation Plan with a trainer or coach. These forms plus a model may also be found at the back of the workbook.

TRAINING LOG

Date *March 9*   Location *Gym/field*

Hours of sleep: *9 ½*   Body weight: *152*   Health: *+*   Hydration: *0*

Nutrition: Grains *4*   Veggies *2*   Fruits *1*   Protein *4*

Activities:

Jog	Intensity Level *2*	Time: *15:00 (1 ½ miles)*
Stretches	Intensity Level *1*	Time: *10:00*
Short toss	Intensity Level *1*	Time: *10:00*
Long toss	Intensity Level *1/2*	Time: *10:00*
Infield	Intensity Level *2*	Time: *20:00*
Batting cage	Intensity Level *1/2*	Time: *10:00*
Stretches	Intensity Level *1*	Time: *10:00*

Total Training Time: *1:25*   Total Season Time: *1:25 + 15:30= 16:55*

Other activities: *Watch Red Sox v. Twins --write Competition Analysis*

Notes on Training: *Swings feel off in batting cage. Ask coach watch me in the batting cage.*

To-do Lists

Sport: Studies/Work:
ICE   *History paper due Friday*
Get a water bottle   *Field trip form*
                                  English Project w/ group

[+]   Today's Training Experience

Figure 3   Baseball infielder's Training Log

It's Your Workbook

If your coach has given you this workbook, the two of you should discuss ways to adapt the book to work more effectively for you. If you're keeping this workbook on your own, follow your instincts and do what works best for you. Always feel free to swap a prompt for one in the back of the book or write about something other than sports. It is your workbook.

Why we write

"Writing organizes and clarifies our thoughts. Writing is how we think our way into a subject and make it our own. Writing enables us to find out what we know—and what we don't know—about whatever we're trying to learn."

–William Zinsser, *Writing to Learn*

Preseason Thoughts,
Athletic Journal Prompts,
& Training Logs

Preseason Thoughts

The prompts below will guide you in thinking back to the previous sports season. You'll also have an opportunity to look closely at the training you have accomplished for this new season. In "Other Thoughts," athletes write about whatever is uppermost in their minds, athletic or not.

What were your strengths last season as an athlete?

What were your weaknesses last season as an athlete?

In the offseason what did you do to improve upon last season's weaknesses?

What are your Personal Goals for this season? A personal goal is not about winning or losing. It's a specific performance goal you hope to accomplish. For example, perhaps you plan to improve your foul shooting percentage in basketball. Your entry would look like this one:

Personal Athletic Goals	What will you do to reach your Personal Athletic Goals?	Who might help you reach these goals?
1. Raise my foul shooting % in basketball by 10%.	1. I used to take 50 foul shots each day. Now, I take a minimum of 75 foul shots at home each day.	1. My little brother Bailey will help if I do the same for him.

Personal Athletic Goals	What will you do to reach your Personal Athletic Goals?	Who might help you reach these goals?
1.	1.	1.
2.	2.	2.
3.	3.	3.

If you're on a team, respond to the following prompts:

Last year our team strengths included...

Last year our team weaknesses included...

Write about your best personal performance last season. What contributed to your success?

Write about your worst performance last season. What contributed to your weakness?

What are you most looking forward to this season and why?

Training Priorities: List three training priorities for this athletic season (e.g., watch more next-level competitions). Then write up to three specific areas you plan to focus on under each priority:

Training Priority #1 _____

    a.

    b.

    c.

Training Priority #2 _____

    a.

    b.

    c.

Training Priority #3 _____

    a.

    b.

    c.

Competition Priorities: List three competition priorities for this athletic season (e.g., study my opponent more thoroughly). Then write up to three specific areas you plan to focus on under each priority:

Competition Priority #1 _____
    a.

    b.

    c.

Competition Priority #2 _____
    a.

    b.

    c.

Competition Priority #3 _____
    a.

    b.

    c.

Notes:

_____

_____

_____

_____

_____

_____

_____

Day 1   *Date*_____

Training

What makes training hard for you?

What makes training easy for you?

Training Log #1

Date_____   Location_____

Hours of sleep: _____ Body weight: _____ Health: _____ Hydration: _____

Nutrition: Grains: _____Veggies: _____ Fruits: _____ Protein: _____

Activities:

_____ Intensity Level: _____   Time: _____

_____ Intensity Level: _____   Time: _____

_____ Intensity Level: _____   Time: _____

_____ Intensity Level: _____   Time: _____

_____ Intensity Level: _____   Time: _____

_____ Intensity Level: _____   Time: _____

_____ Intensity Level: _____   Time: _____

Total Training Time: _____ Total Season Time: _____

Other activities:

_____

Notes on Training:

_____
_____
_____

To-do Lists:

Sport: Studies/Work:

_____   _____

_____   _____

_____   _____

_____   _____

☐ Today's Training Experience

Day 2   Date_____

Your Timeline as an Athlete

Create a timeline of your athletic career. Include your athletic milestones, important coaches, and different teams or competition levels. Write above and below the timeline.

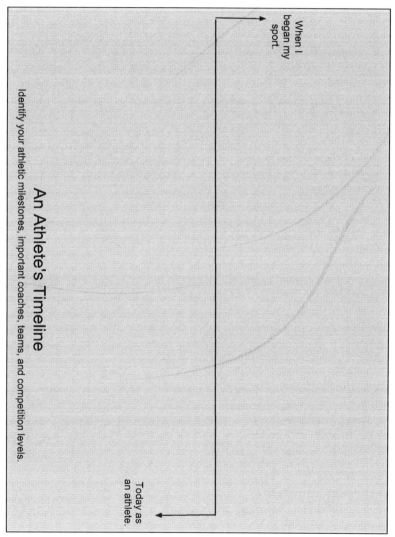

What's one thing you've noticed or thought about while filling out this timeline?

Training Log #2

Date_____   Location_____

Hours of sleep: _____ Body weight: _____ Health: _____ Hydration: _____

Nutrition: Grains: _____Veggies: _____ Fruits: _____ Protein: _____

Activities:

_____ Intensity Level: _____   Time: _____

_____ Intensity Level: _____   Time: _____

_____ Intensity Level: _____   Time: _____

_____ Intensity Level: _____   Time: _____

_____ Intensity Level: _____   Time: _____

_____ Intensity Level: _____   Time: _____

_____ Intensity Level: _____   Time: _____

Total Training Time: _____ Total Season Time: _____

Other activities:
_____

Notes on Training:
_____
_____
_____

To-do Lists:

Sport: Studies/Work:

_____   _____

_____   _____

_____   _____

_____   _____

☐ Today's Training Experience

Day 3 *Date*_____

An Effective Coach

List up to five qualities of an effective coach:

1. _____

2. _____

3. _____

4. _____

5. _____

Tell the story of a good moment during a competition or training session with one of your coaches:

Training Log #3

Date_____   Location_____

Hours of sleep: _____ Body weight: _____ Health: _____ Hydration: _____

Nutrition: Grains: _____ Veggies: _____ Fruits: _____ Protein: _____

Activities:

_____ Intensity Level: _____   Time: _____

_____ Intensity Level: _____   Time: _____

_____ Intensity Level: _____   Time: _____

_____ Intensity Level: _____   Time: _____

_____ Intensity Level: _____   Time: _____

_____ Intensity Level: _____   Time: _____

_____ Intensity Level: _____   Time: _____

Total Training Time: _____ Total Season Time: _____

Other activities:
_____

Notes on Training:
_____
_____
_____

To-do Lists:

Sport: Studies/Work:

_____   _____

_____   _____

_____   _____

_____   _____

[ ]   Today's Training Experience

Day 4   *Date*_____

The Perfect Warm-Up

Outline your perfect warm-up routine before a training session. Include the approximate amount of time you spend on each activity, your target heart rate using the Training Intensity Levels from the Introduction (usually, you'll warm up at a 1 or a 1/2), and the reason you have included this activity.

Warm-up activity	Time	Intensity Level (1,2,3)	Why this activity?

Training Log #4

Date_____   Location_____

Hours of sleep: _____ Body weight: _____ Health: _____ Hydration: _____

Nutrition: Grains: _____Veggies: _____ Fruits: _____ Protein: _____

Activities:

_____ Intensity Level: _____   Time: _____

_____ Intensity Level: _____   Time: _____

_____ Intensity Level: _____   Time: _____

_____ Intensity Level: _____   Time: _____

_____ Intensity Level: _____   Time: _____

_____ Intensity Level: _____   Time: _____

_____ Intensity Level: _____   Time: _____

Total Training Time: _____ Total Season Time: _____

Other activities:

_____

Notes on Training:

_____
_____
_____

To-do Lists:

Sport: Studies/Work:

_____   _____

_____   _____

_____   _____

_____   _____

Today's Training Experience

Day 5   Date_____

Write about your favorite training partner.

Name_____

Qualities as an athlete:

Qualities as a person:

Unique habits or quirks:

Best story about your training partner:

What have you learned from this athlete?

Training Log #5

Date_____   Location_____

Hours of sleep: _____ Body weight: _____ Health: _____ Hydration: _____

Nutrition: Grains: _____Veggies: _____ Fruits: _____ Protein: _____

Activities:

_____ Intensity Level: _____   Time: _____

_____ Intensity Level: _____   Time: _____

_____ Intensity Level: _____   Time: _____

_____ Intensity Level: _____   Time: _____

_____ Intensity Level: _____   Time: _____

_____ Intensity Level: _____   Time: _____

_____ Intensity Level: _____   Time: _____

Total Training Time: _____ Total Season Time: _____

Other activities:
_____

Notes on Training:
_____
_____
_____

To-do Lists:

Sport: Studies/Work:

_____   _____

_____   _____

_____   _____

_____   _____

Today's Training Experience

Day 6   *Date_____*

Describe a perfect training session or practice.

Where would it be? Who would attend? How long would it last? What activities would occur? Have you ever experienced perfection in a training session or practice? Write about that, too.

Training Log #6

Date_____   Location_____

Hours of sleep: _____ Body weight: _____ Health: _____ Hydration: _____

Nutrition: Grains: _____Veggies: _____ Fruits: _____ Protein: _____

Activities:

_____ Intensity Level: _____   Time: _____

_____ Intensity Level: _____   Time: _____

_____ Intensity Level: _____   Time: _____

_____ Intensity Level: _____   Time: _____

_____ Intensity Level: _____   Time: _____

_____ Intensity Level: _____   Time: _____

_____ Intensity Level: _____   Time: _____

Total Training Time: _____ Total Season Time: _____

Other activities:
_____

Notes on Training:
_____
_____
_____

To-do Lists:

Sport: Studies/Work:

_____   _____

_____   _____

_____   _____

_____   _____

☐   Today's Training Experience

Day 7 *Date*_____

Who brings out your best and why?

Who brings out the best in you as an athlete and why? You might first think of a coach, manager, or trainer. But also think about family members, fans, teammates, or even an opponent.

Training Log #7

Date_____   Location_____

Hours of sleep: _____ Body weight: _____ Health: _____ Hydration: _____

Nutrition: Grains: _____ Veggies: _____ Fruits: _____ Protein: _____

Activities:

_____ Intensity Level: _____   Time: _____

_____ Intensity Level: _____   Time: _____

_____ Intensity Level: _____   Time: _____

_____ Intensity Level: _____   Time: _____

_____ Intensity Level: _____   Time: _____

_____ Intensity Level: _____   Time: _____

_____ Intensity Level: _____   Time: _____

Total Training Time: _____ Total Season Time: _____

Other activities:
_____

Notes on Training:
_____
_____
_____

To-do Lists:

Sport: Studies/Work:

_____   _____

_____   _____

_____   _____

_____   _____

☐   Today's Training Experience

$Day \ 8$ *Date*_____

Unpacking Your Training Days

Using the past 7 days of your training, look back in your log and fill out the following:

What's your total training time? _____ Average nightly hours of sleep: _____

Hydration Assessment: How many _____ (+) _____ (O) _____ (–)

Training Day Assessment: How many _____ (+) _____ (O) _____ (–)

What have you done well during your first 7 days of training?

What do you think you need to improve upon?

Go back through your first seven training days and read each "Notes on Training." Take one word or phrase from each comment you've written and place them below (if you didn't write anything on a particular day, just leave the line blank):

Day 1 _____

Day 2 _____

Day 3 _____

Day 4 _____

Day 5 _____

Day 6 _____

Day 7 _____

What does this list of words tell you about your training?

Assess (√) your first week of training: _____ (+)_____ (O) _____ (–)

Training Log #8

Date_____ Location_____

Hours of sleep: _____ Body weight: _____ Health: _____ Hydration: _____

Nutrition: Grains: _____ Veggies: _____ Fruits: _____ Protein: _____

Activities:

_____ Intensity Level: _____ Time: _____

_____ Intensity Level: _____ Time: _____

_____ Intensity Level: _____ Time: _____

_____ Intensity Level: _____ Time: _____

_____ Intensity Level: _____ Time: _____

_____ Intensity Level: _____ Time: _____

_____ Intensity Level: _____ Time: _____

Total Training Time: _____ Total Season Time: _____

Other activities:
_____

Notes on Training:
_____
_____
_____

To-do Lists:

Sport: Studies/Work:

_____   _____

_____   _____

_____   _____

_____   _____

Today's Training Experience

Day 9   Date_____

Making Meaning Activity: *Training*

Step #1: List some of the words that come to mind when you think about "training." Place the words in the chart below.

Step #2: Name the opposite of the words in Step One. Looking at both sides of any topic (i.e., true/false, positive/negative, right/wrong) can help us come to know a topic more fully.

Step #1 *Example: easy*	Step #2 *Example: hard*

Step #3: Write two sentences about training using two pair of the opposing words form above. For example: *Some days training is* easy *because I feel strong; other days training is* difficult, *and I feel like I'm going backwards and getting weaker.*

Step #4: Write a 5-sentence paragraph about training using the guidelines below. This exercise will help you find your "truth" about training.

Sentence 1	a five-word statement
Sentence 2	a question
Sentence 3	two independent clauses combined by a semi-colon
Sentence 4	a sentence with an introductory phrase
Sentence 5	a two-word statement

Training Log #9

Date_____   Location_____

Hours of sleep: _____ Body weight: _____ Health: _____ Hydration: _____

Nutrition: Grains: _____Veggies: _____ Fruits: _____ Protein: _____

Activities:

_____ Intensity Level: _____   Time: _____

_____ Intensity Level: _____   Time: _____

_____ Intensity Level: _____   Time: _____

_____ Intensity Level: _____   Time: _____

_____ Intensity Level: _____   Time: _____

_____ Intensity Level: _____   Time: _____

_____ Intensity Level: _____   Time: _____

Total Training Time: _____ Total Season Time: _____

Other activities:
_____

Notes on Training:
_____
_____
_____

To-do Lists:

Sport: Studies/Work:

_____   _____

_____   _____

_____   _____

_____   _____

Today's Training Experience

Day 10 *Date_____*

Rapid Response

Write a quick response and a reason why for each:

My favorite training food is...

In my sport, I am frightened about...

My favorite exercise during training is...

When I win a competition by a wide margin, I ...
–or–
If I ever won a competition by a wide margin, I ...

When my coach says _____ I feel like ....

Training Log #10

Date_____   Location_____

Hours of sleep: _____ Body weight: _____ Health: _____ Hydration: _____

Nutrition: Grains: _____Veggies: _____ Fruits: _____ Protein: _____

Activities:

_____ Intensity Level: _____   Time: _____

_____ Intensity Level: _____   Time: _____

_____ Intensity Level: _____   Time: _____

_____ Intensity Level: _____   Time: _____

_____ Intensity Level: _____   Time: _____

_____ Intensity Level: _____   Time: _____

_____ Intensity Level: _____   Time: _____

Total Training Time: _____ Total Season Time: _____

Other activities:
_____

Notes on Training:
_____
_____
_____

To-do Lists:

Sport: Studies/Work:

_____   _____

_____   _____

_____   _____

_____   _____

Today's Training Experience

Day 11 *Date*_____

Photo Story

Use your imagination and tell the story of these four soccer players. (If you'd like to know the real story behind the photo, see page 2 of *Writing on the Bus.*)

Training Log #11

Date_____   Location_____

Hours of sleep: _____ Body weight: _____ Health: _____ Hydration: _____

Nutrition: Grains: _____Veggies: _____ Fruits: _____ Protein: _____

Activities:

_____ Intensity Level: _____   Time: _____

_____ Intensity Level: _____   Time: _____

_____ Intensity Level: _____   Time: _____

_____ Intensity Level: _____   Time: _____

_____ Intensity Level: _____   Time: _____

_____ Intensity Level: _____   Time: _____

_____ Intensity Level: _____   Time: _____

Total Training Time: _____ Total Season Time: _____

Other activities:
_____

Notes on Training:
_____
_____
_____

To-do Lists:

Sport: Studies/Work:

_____   _____

_____   _____

_____   _____

_____   _____

Today's Training Experience

Day 12 *Date*_____

Injury or Illness

You just sprained an ankle or know you're coming down with an illness like a cold or the flu. What's the first thing you do? Who do you speak with? Think and write about how you organize yourself to get through an injury or illness.

Training Log #12

Date_____   Location_____

Hours of sleep: _____ Body weight: _____ Health: _____ Hydration: _____

Nutrition: Grains: _____Veggies: _____ Fruits: _____ Protein: _____

Activities:

_____ Intensity Level: _____   Time: _____

_____ Intensity Level: _____   Time: _____

_____ Intensity Level: _____   Time: _____

_____ Intensity Level: _____   Time: _____

_____ Intensity Level: _____   Time: _____

_____ Intensity Level: _____   Time: _____

_____ Intensity Level: _____   Time: _____

Total Training Time: _____ Total Season Time: _____

Other activities:
_____

Notes on Training:
_____
_____
_____

To-do Lists:

Sport: Studies/Work:

_____   _____

_____   _____

_____   _____

_____   _____

Today's Training Experience

Day 13 *Date*_____

Proudest Moment

Other than winning a competition, tell the story of your proudest moment as an athlete.

Training Log #13

Date_____   Location_____

Hours of sleep: _____ Body weight: _____ Health: _____ Hydration: _____

Nutrition: Grains: _____Veggies: _____ Fruits: _____ Protein: _____

Activities:

_____ Intensity Level: _____   Time: _____

_____ Intensity Level: _____   Time: _____

_____ Intensity Level: _____   Time: _____

_____ Intensity Level: _____   Time: _____

_____ Intensity Level: _____   Time: _____

_____ Intensity Level: _____   Time: _____

_____ Intensity Level: _____   Time: _____

Total Training Time: _____ Total Season Time: _____

Other activities:
_____

Notes on Training:
_____
_____
_____

To-do Lists:

Sport: Studies/Work:

_____   _____

_____   _____

_____   _____

_____   _____

Today's Training Experience

Day 14  *Date*_____

Photo Thoughts

Paste a picture of yourself from a competition or training session in the space below. The photo could be from a newspaper clipping or Facebook.

Write about what you see, feel, or think about when you look at this photograph.

Training Log #14

Date_____   Location_____

Hours of sleep: _____ Body weight: _____ Health: _____ Hydration: _____

Nutrition: Grains: _____Veggies: _____ Fruits: _____ Protein: _____

Activities:

_____ Intensity Level: _____   Time: _____

_____ Intensity Level: _____   Time: _____

_____ Intensity Level: _____   Time: _____

_____ Intensity Level: _____   Time: _____

_____ Intensity Level: _____   Time: _____

_____ Intensity Level: _____   Time: _____

_____ Intensity Level: _____   Time: _____

Total Training Time: _____ Total Season Time: _____

Other activities:
_____

Notes on Training:
_____
_____
_____

To-do Lists:

Sport: Studies/Work:

_____   _____

_____   _____

_____   _____

_____   _____

Today's Training Experience

Day 15 *Date*_____

T-shirt Slogans

Come up with four t-shirt slogans/sayings about competing or training, your sport or team. Use the t-shirts provided. Here are a few slogans/sayings to jumpstart your thinking:

Got VO^2 Max?   *Train Here, Train Now*   *Max Out.*
Live at the Threshold.   *Yeah, training.*   *Go train yourself.*

Training Log #15

Date_____   Location_____

Hours of sleep: _____ Body weight: _____ Health: _____ Hydration: _____

Nutrition: Grains: _____Veggies: _____ Fruits: _____ Protein: _____

Activities:

_____ Intensity Level: _____   Time: _____

_____ Intensity Level: _____   Time: _____

_____ Intensity Level: _____   Time: _____

_____ Intensity Level: _____   Time: _____

_____ Intensity Level: _____   Time: _____

_____ Intensity Level: _____   Time: _____

_____ Intensity Level: _____   Time: _____

Total Training Time: _____ Total Season Time: _____

Other activities:

_____

Notes on Training:

_____
_____
_____

To-do Lists:

Sport: Studies/Work:

_____   _____

_____   _____

_____   _____

_____   _____

Today's Training Experience

Day 16 Date_____

Competition Analysis II
(See page 10 for more information on the Competition Analysis II.)

Team/Athlete #1_____   Team/Athlete #2_____

Strengths: Strengths:

Weaknesses: Weaknesses:

Adjustments at the halfway point: Adjustments at the halfway point:

Comparisons: If you watched two football teams, compare their offenses and defenses, their quarterbacks, linesmen, and receivers. If you watched two tennis players, compare the players' service games, net points, or composure. If you watched a road race, select two favorite runners and discuss issues such as their strategies, stride, and fitness:

Describe the critical moment of the competition:

Final Analysis: Think as a coach about strengths and/or weaknesses (e.g., athleticism, speed, coaching, motivation/ heart). What adjustments might you have suggested to either team/athlete if you were the coach?

Training Log #16

Date_____   Location_____

Hours of sleep: _____ Body weight: _____ Health: _____ Hydration: _____

Nutrition: Grains: _____Veggies: _____ Fruits: _____ Protein: _____

Activities:

_____ Intensity Level: _____   Time: _____

_____ Intensity Level: _____   Time: _____

_____ Intensity Level: _____   Time: _____

_____ Intensity Level: _____   Time: _____

_____ Intensity Level: _____   Time: _____

_____ Intensity Level: _____   Time: _____

_____ Intensity Level: _____   Time: _____

Total Training Time: _____ Total Season Time: _____

Other activities:

_____

Notes on Training:

_____
_____
_____

To-do Lists:

Sport: Studies/Work:

_____   _____

_____   _____

_____   _____

_____   _____

☐ Today's Training Experience e

Day 17 *Date*_____

"Do or do not. There is no try."

–Yoda

What might these words from Jedi Master Yoda of Star Wars have to do with sports?

Training Log #17

Date_____   Location_____

Hours of sleep: _____ Body weight: _____ Health: _____ Hydration: _____

Nutrition: Grains: _____Veggies: _____ Fruits: _____ Protein: _____

Activities:

_____ Intensity Level: _____   Time: _____

_____ Intensity Level: _____   Time: _____

_____ Intensity Level: _____   Time: _____

_____ Intensity Level: _____   Time: _____

_____ Intensity Level: _____   Time: _____

_____ Intensity Level: _____   Time: _____

_____ Intensity Level: _____   Time: _____

Total Training Time: _____ Total Season Time: _____

Other activities:

_____

Notes on Training:

_____
_____
_____

To-do Lists:

Sport: Studies/Work:

_____   _____

_____   _____

_____   _____

_____   _____

Today's Training Experience

Day 18 *Date*_____

Posers

Write about an athlete who is a "poser." Why do you think this happens to some athletes?

When, if ever, have you come close to being a poser? Why do you think it happened to you?

Training Log #18

Date_____   Location_____

Hours of sleep: _____ Body weight: _____ Health: _____ Hydration: _____

Nutrition: Grains: _____ Veggies: _____ Fruits: _____ Protein: _____

Activities:

_____ Intensity Level: _____   Time: _____

_____ Intensity Level: _____   Time: _____

_____ Intensity Level: _____   Time: _____

_____ Intensity Level: _____   Time: _____

_____ Intensity Level: _____   Time: _____

_____ Intensity Level: _____   Time: _____

_____ Intensity Level: _____   Time: _____

Total Training Time: _____ Total Season Time: _____

Other activities:
_____

Notes on Training:
_____
_____
_____

To-do Lists:

Sport: Studies/Work:

_____   _____

_____   _____

_____   _____

_____   _____

Today's Training Experience

Day 19 Date_____

Draw Yourself...

Draw a picture of yourself after a good performance. Write a caption.

Caption_____

Training Log #19

Date_____   Location_____

Hours of sleep: _____ Body weight: _____ Health: _____ Hydration: _____

Nutrition: Grains: _____Veggies: _____ Fruits: _____ Protein: _____

Activities:

_____ Intensity Level: _____   Time: _____

_____ Intensity Level: _____   Time: _____

_____ Intensity Level: _____   Time: _____

_____ Intensity Level: _____   Time: _____

_____ Intensity Level: _____   Time: _____

_____ Intensity Level: _____   Time: _____

_____ Intensity Level: _____   Time: _____

Total Training Time: _____ Total Season Time: _____

Other activities:
_____

Notes on Training:
_____
_____
_____

To-do Lists:

Sport: Studies/Work:

_____   _____

_____   _____

_____   _____

_____   _____

Today's Training Experience

Day 20 *Date*_____

Advice

What advice or talk do you <u>least</u> like to hear before an important competition and why?

Training Log #20

Date_____   Location_____

Hours of sleep: _____ Body weight: _____ Health: _____ Hydration: _____

Nutrition: Grains: _____Veggies: _____ Fruits: _____ Protein: _____

Activities:

_____ Intensity Level: _____   Time: _____

_____ Intensity Level: _____   Time: _____

_____ Intensity Level: _____   Time: _____

_____ Intensity Level: _____   Time: _____

_____ Intensity Level: _____   Time: _____

_____ Intensity Level: _____   Time: _____

_____ Intensity Level: _____   Time: _____

Total Training Time: _____ Total Season Time: _____

Other activities:
_____

Notes on Training:
_____
_____
_____

To-do Lists:

Sport: Studies/Work:

_____   _____

_____   _____

_____   _____

_____   _____

[ ]   Today's Training Experience

Day 21 _Date_____ _____

World-Class Thoughts

Here are some of the themes from the journal of an elite, world-class athlete who was thirty years old:

Loneliness	Relaxation	Lists
Training	Breathing	Equipment
Family	Preparation	Sponsors
Friends	Control	Balance
Focus	Routine	Alignment
Emotions	Yoga	Symmetry
Food	Writing	Asserting
Dreams	Need for	oneself
Body Tension	success	Satisfaction
Colors	Self-esteem	Optimism
Visualization	Playfulness	Goals
Awareness	Schedules	

First, what comes to mind when you read this list?

Second, select one of the themes. Write about the theme for 2-3 minutes and how it relates to you as an athlete.

Training Log #21

Date_____   Location_____

Hours of sleep: _____ Body weight: _____ Health: _____ Hydration: _____

Nutrition: Grains: _____Veggies: _____ Fruits: _____ Protein: _____

Activities:

_____ Intensity Level: _____   Time: _____

_____ Intensity Level: _____   Time: _____

_____ Intensity Level: _____   Time: _____

_____ Intensity Level: _____   Time: _____

_____ Intensity Level: _____   Time: _____

_____ Intensity Level: _____   Time: _____

_____ Intensity Level: _____   Time: _____

Total Training Time: _____ Total Season Time: _____

Other activities:
_____

Notes on Training:
_____
_____
_____

To-do Lists:

Sport: Studies/Work:

_____   _____

_____   _____

_____   _____

_____   _____

Today's Training Experience

Day 22 *Date*_____

Three-Week Analysis

Using the *above average* (+), *average* (O), and *below average* (–) ratings from the past three weeks, draw three line graphs for your health, hydration, and training experiences. What do these graphs tell you? Here's a model of 21 days of Training Experiences taken from the box at the bottom of each Training Log:

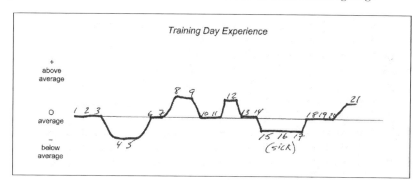

Hydration

+

0 ~~~~~~

–

Health

+

0 ~~~~~~

–

Training

+

0 ~~~~~~

–

Training Log #22

Date_____   Location_____

Hours of sleep: _____ Body weight: _____ Health: _____ Hydration: _____

Nutrition: Grains: _____ Veggies: _____ Fruits: _____ Protein: _____

Activities:

_____ Intensity Level: _____   Time: _____

_____ Intensity Level: _____   Time: _____

_____ Intensity Level: _____   Time: _____

_____ Intensity Level: _____   Time: _____

_____ Intensity Level: _____   Time: _____

_____ Intensity Level: _____   Time: _____

_____ Intensity Level: _____   Time: _____

Total Training Time: _____ Total Season Time: _____

Other activities: _____

Notes on Training:

_____
_____
_____

To-do Lists:

Sport: Studies/Work:

_____   _____

_____   _____

_____   _____

_____   _____

Today's Training Experience

Day 23 *Date*_____

Performance Analysis

Some days before competing you feel "on." You're ready to have at it and everything is in sync. Some days... not so much. Why is that? What affects your performance? Food, friends, sleep, the opponent, your coach, your mood, or the wrong socks? Make two lists of what may influence your competitive performances, good and bad.

Good Competition *Sample: I know my opponent.*	Bad Competition *Sample: I lack confidence*

Write one or two sentences that capture your thinking about the lists above:

Training Log #23

Date_____   Location_____

Hours of sleep: _____ Body weight: _____ Health: _____ Hydration: _____

Nutrition: Grains: _____ Veggies: _____ Fruits: _____ Protein: _____

Activities:

_____ Intensity Level: _____   Time: _____

_____ Intensity Level: _____   Time: _____

_____ Intensity Level: _____   Time: _____

_____ Intensity Level: _____   Time: _____

_____ Intensity Level: _____   Time: _____

_____ Intensity Level: _____   Time: _____

_____ Intensity Level: _____   Time: _____

Total Training Time: _____ Total Season Time:
_____

Other activities: _____

Notes on Training:
_____
_____
_____

To-do Lists:

Sport: Studies/Work:

_____   _____

_____   _____

_____   _____

_____   _____

Today's Training Experience

Day 24 *Date*_____

When you were young...

When you were young, whom did you admire as an athlete and why?

Training Log #24

Date_____   Location_____

Hours of sleep: _____ Body weight: _____ Health: _____ Hydration: _____

Nutrition: Grains: _____Veggies: _____ Fruits: _____ Protein: _____

Activities:

_____ Intensity Level: _____   Time: _____

_____ Intensity Level: _____   Time: _____

_____ Intensity Level: _____   Time: _____

_____ Intensity Level: _____   Time: _____

_____ Intensity Level: _____   Time: _____

_____ Intensity Level: _____   Time: _____

_____ Intensity Level: _____   Time: _____

Total Training Time: _____ Total Season Time: _____

Other activities: _____

Notes on Training:
_____
_____
_____

To-do Lists:

Sport: Studies/Work:

_____   _____

_____   _____

_____   _____

_____   _____

Today's Training Experience

Day 25 *Date*_____

Writing a Game, Race, Meet, or Match

Tell the story of one of your games or competitions. Let's say you run 10k road races. Write about your pre-race routine all the way through to your cool down. Remember to write about the nitty-gritty like what you ate, how long you warmed up, what you visualized before the race, what you "said" to yourself as you stepped to the start, thoughts at different stages of the race, pacing strategy, the effect of other runners on your race, recovery...

Training Log #25

Date_____   Location_____

Hours of sleep: _____ Body weight: _____ Health: _____ Hydration: _____

Nutrition: Grains: _____Veggies: _____ Fruits: _____ Protein: _____

Activities:

_____ Intensity Level: _____   Time: _____

_____ Intensity Level: _____   Time: _____

_____ Intensity Level: _____   Time: _____

_____ Intensity Level: _____   Time: _____

_____ Intensity Level: _____   Time: _____

_____ Intensity Level: _____   Time: _____

_____ Intensity Level: _____   Time: _____

Total Training Time: _____ Total Season Time: _____

Other activities: _____

Notes on Training:
_____
_____
_____

To-do Lists:

Sport: Studies/Work:

_____   _____

_____   _____

_____   _____

_____   _____

Today's Training Experience

Day 26 *Date*_____

Letter to a Former Coach

Write a letter to one of your former coaches. You may wish to include some of the following: what you're doing now as an athlete; the coach's contributions to your athletic and personal life; the issues you currently face as an athlete; a fun memory; and a photo.

Training Log #26

Date_____ Location_____

Hours of sleep: _____ Body weight: _____ Health: _____ Hydration: _____

Nutrition: Grains: _____Veggies: _____ Fruits: _____ Protein: _____

Activities:

_____ Intensity Level: _____ Time: _____

_____ Intensity Level: _____ Time: _____

_____ Intensity Level: _____ Time: _____

_____ Intensity Level: _____ Time: _____

_____ Intensity Level: _____ Time: _____

_____ Intensity Level: _____ Time: _____

_____ Intensity Level: _____ Time: _____

Total Training Time: _____ Total Season Time: _____

Other activities: _____

Notes on Training:

_____
_____
_____

To-do Lists:

Sport: Studies/Work:

_____   _____

_____   _____

_____   _____

_____   _____

Today's Training Experience

Day 27 *Date*_____

Instructional Video

Watch an instructional video on your sport. You will be able to find many online (e.g., YouTube.com). Write about the following prompts:

~Title of Video and website address:

~New information you learned:

~Questions you had after watching the videos:

~Ideas you might share with a fellow athlete:

~Knowledge you might share with a coach:

~Suggestions you'd make for revising the video:

Training Log #27

Date_____   Location_____

Hours of sleep: _____ Body weight: _____ Health: _____ Hydration: _____

Nutrition: Grains: _____Veggies: _____ Fruits: _____ Protein: _____

Activities:

_____ Intensity Level: _____   Time: _____

_____ Intensity Level: _____   Time: _____

_____ Intensity Level: _____   Time: _____

_____ Intensity Level: _____   Time: _____

_____ Intensity Level: _____   Time: _____

_____ Intensity Level: _____   Time: _____

_____ Intensity Level: _____   Time: _____

Total Training Time: _____ Total Season Time: _____

Other activities: _____

Notes on Training:

_____
_____
_____

To-do Lists:

Sport: Studies/Work:

_____   _____
_____   _____
_____   _____
_____   _____

Today's Training Experience

Day 28 *Date*_____

A Letter to a Teammate

Write a letter to a teammate or fellow athlete, past or present.

Training Log #28

Date_____   Location_____

Hours of sleep: _____ Body weight: _____ Health: _____ Hydration: _____

Nutrition: Grains: _____Veggies: _____ Fruits: _____ Protein: _____

Activities:

_____ Intensity Level: _____   Time: _____

_____ Intensity Level: _____   Time: _____

_____ Intensity Level: _____   Time: _____

_____ Intensity Level: _____   Time: _____

_____ Intensity Level: _____   Time: _____

_____ Intensity Level: _____   Time: _____

_____ Intensity Level: _____   Time: _____

Total Training Time: _____ Total Season Time: _____

Other activities: _____

Notes on Training:

_____
_____
_____

To-do Lists:

Sport: Studies/Work:

_____   _____
_____   _____
_____   _____
_____   _____

Today's Training Experience

Day 29 *Date*_____

Three-Sentence Poem

Using the words, images, actions, or moments from your sport, write a poem using the following template. Don't forget to include a title. The idea for a three-sentence poem came from the book *A Surge of Language* (Wormser & Cappella, 2004).

Directions:

1st sentence: a setting or action
2nd sentence: question
3rd sentence: an image

Example:

LAST PLAY

A stiff breeze,
four quarters of a solid ground game
and an all-conference back
set the play.

Is the fake taken?

Alone in the end zone...
the ball spirals true to mark—
he drops it and
awakes to the championship
he lost.

Training Log #29

Date_____   Location_____

Hours of sleep: _____ Body weight: _____ Health: _____ Hydration: _____

Nutrition: Grains: _____Veggies: _____ Fruits: _____ Protein: _____

Activities:

_____ Intensity Level: _____   Time: _____

_____ Intensity Level: _____   Time: _____

_____ Intensity Level: _____   Time: _____

_____ Intensity Level: _____   Time: _____

_____ Intensity Level: _____   Time: _____

_____ Intensity Level: _____   Time: _____

_____ Intensity Level: _____   Time: _____

Total Training Time: _____ Total Season Time: _____

Other activities: _____

Notes on Training:

_____
_____
_____

To-do Lists:

Sport: Studies/Work:

_____   _____
_____   _____
_____   _____
_____   _____

Today's Training Experience

Day 30 Date_____

The Advantages of Doing Poorly

Why can this statement be true: "Some days, doing poorly is the most important result that could happen." Give examples from your own work as an athlete.

Training Log #30

Date_____   Location_____

Hours of sleep: _____ Body weight: _____ Health: _____ Hydration: _____

Nutrition: Grains: _____Veggies: _____ Fruits: _____ Protein: _____

Activities:

_____ Intensity Level: _____   Time: _____

_____ Intensity Level: _____   Time: _____

_____ Intensity Level: _____   Time: _____

_____ Intensity Level: _____   Time: _____

_____ Intensity Level: _____   Time: _____

_____ Intensity Level: _____   Time: _____

_____ Intensity Level: _____   Time: _____

Total Training Time: _____ Total Season Time: _____

Other activities: _____

Notes on Training:

_____
_____
_____

To-do Lists:

Sport: Studies/Work:

_____   _____
_____   _____
_____   _____
_____   _____

Today's Training Experience

Day 31 *Date_____*

Favorite Sports Movie

What's your favorite sports movie of all time and why? What do you like about the movie? Do you relate to any of the characters? Would you recommend this movie to a younger athlete? If so, why?

Training Log #31

Date_____   Location_____

Hours of sleep: _____ Body weight: _____ Health: _____ Hydration: _____

Nutrition: Grains: _____Veggies: _____ Fruits: _____ Protein: _____

Activities:

_____ Intensity Level: _____   Time: _____

_____ Intensity Level: _____   Time: _____

_____ Intensity Level: _____   Time: _____

_____ Intensity Level: _____   Time: _____

_____ Intensity Level: _____   Time: _____

_____ Intensity Level: _____   Time: _____

_____ Intensity Level: _____   Time: _____

Total Training Time: _____ Total Season Time: _____

Other activities: _____

Notes on Training:

_____
_____
_____

To-do Lists:

Sport: Studies/Work:

_____   _____

_____   _____

_____   _____

_____   _____

Today's Training Experience

Day 32 Date_____

Tag a Teammate or Fellow Athlete

Under each category, name a teammate or fellow athlete. Give an example or two of the athlete's qualities.

Tag a Teammate

Who'd make a great coach?	A true sportsman	Dedication plus	Kindest
Most coachable	Always leaves it on the field	Most motivating	Great future
Great opponent	Team Leader	Fun	Positive
Healthy	Student-Athlete: the complete package	Who should take the last shot	Fitness Fanatic

Training Log #32

Date_____   Location_____

Hours of sleep: _____ Body weight: _____ Health: _____ Hydration: _____

Nutrition: Grains: _____Veggies: _____ Fruits: _____ Protein: _____

Activities:

_____ Intensity Level: _____   Time: _____

_____ Intensity Level: _____   Time: _____

_____ Intensity Level: _____   Time: _____

_____ Intensity Level: _____   Time: _____

_____ Intensity Level: _____   Time: _____

_____ Intensity Level: _____   Time: _____

_____ Intensity Level: _____   Time: _____

Total Training Time: _____ Total Season Time: _____

Other activities: _____

Notes on Training:

_____
_____
_____

To-do Lists:

Sport: Studies/Work:

_____   _____

_____   _____

_____   _____

_____   _____

Today's Training Experience

Day 33 *Date*_____

> "It is more important to participate than to win."
> —The Olympic Credo

Write about the Olympic Credo. Why do you think the Olympic Committee adopted this philosophy? Can you give any examples from your own athletic career when you witnessed or experienced this belief in action?

Training Log #33

Date_____   Location_____

Hours of sleep: _____ Body weight: _____ Health: _____ Hydration: _____

Nutrition: Grains: _____Veggies: _____ Fruits: _____ Protein: _____

Activities:

_____ Intensity Level: _____   Time: _____

_____ Intensity Level: _____   Time: _____

_____ Intensity Level: _____   Time: _____

_____ Intensity Level: _____   Time: _____

_____ Intensity Level: _____   Time: _____

_____ Intensity Level: _____   Time: _____

_____ Intensity Level: _____   Time: _____

Total Training Time: _____ Total Season Time: _____

Other activities: _____

Notes on Training:

_____
_____
_____

To-do Lists:

Sport: Studies/Work:

_____   _____

_____   _____

_____   _____

_____   _____

☐   Today's Training Experience

Day 34 Date_____

Packing List

Here's US Ski Racer David Chamberlain's packing list for Europe. If you were leaving for a three-four week tour, what would your packing list include? Make list below.

For my trip:

Equipment	Training Clothes	Casual Clothes	Nutrition	Electronics	Books
Skis (2)	Socks (8)	Jeans (2)	~~Sport Drink~~	Computer	~~...~~
Boots (3)	Undershirts (3)	Sweatshirts (2)	Enduox	I-pod	-?-
Poles (4)	Long underwear bottoms (2)	T's (3)	Bumblebars	~~Palm Pilot~~	-Writing Stuff-
Yoga Mat (1)	Long underwear tops (3)	Nice shirt (2)		Cell	
Pillow (1)	Suits (2)	Underwear (8)		DVD's	
~~Belt~~	Jackets (2)	Long Sleeve shirt (1)		Tapes,	
Sunglasses (3)	Gloves (3)			Tape player	
Drinkbelt (1)	Toys (2)				
Running Shoes (1)	Bike Pants (1)				
Lounging Shoes (1)					

?
___
Waxes

To Buy
→ DVD's
→ Books

83

Training Log #34

Date_____   Location_____

Hours of sleep: _____ Body weight: _____ Health: _____ Hydration: _____

Nutrition: Grains: _____Veggies: _____ Fruits: _____ Protein: _____

Activities:

_____ Intensity Level: _____   Time: _____

_____ Intensity Level: _____   Time: _____

_____ Intensity Level: _____   Time: _____

_____ Intensity Level: _____   Time: _____

_____ Intensity Level: _____   Time: _____

_____ Intensity Level: _____   Time: _____

_____ Intensity Level: _____   Time: _____

Total Training Time: _____ Total Season Time: _____

Other activities: _____

Notes on Training:

_____
_____
_____

To-do Lists:

Sport: Studies/Work:

_____   _____
_____   _____
_____   _____
_____   _____

☐   Today's Training Experience

Day 35 *Date*_____

Stretches

Here are some of David Chamberlain's stretches and Yoga poses.

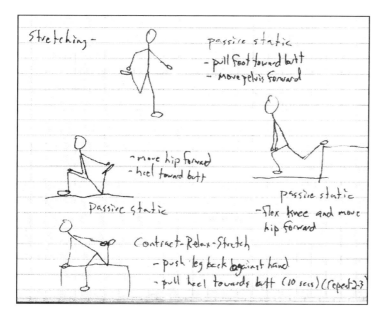

Draw your favorite stretches or Yoga poses:

Training Log #35

Date_____   Location_____

Hours of sleep: _____ Body weight: _____ Health: _____ Hydration: _____

Nutrition: Grains: _____Veggies: _____ Fruits: _____ Protein: _____

Activities:

_____ Intensity Level: _____   Time: _____

_____ Intensity Level: _____   Time: _____

_____ Intensity Level: _____   Time: _____

_____ Intensity Level: _____   Time: _____

_____ Intensity Level: _____   Time: _____

_____ Intensity Level: _____   Time: _____

_____ Intensity Level: _____   Time: _____

Total Training Time: _____ Total Season Time: _____

Other activities: _____

Notes on Training:

_____
_____
_____

To-do Lists:

Sport: Studies/Work:

_____   _____

_____   _____

_____   _____

_____   _____

Today's Training Experience

Day 36 *Date*_____

Midseason Thoughts
Looking back to think forward

The prompts below will guide you in thinking back through your sports season so far. You'll also have an opportunity to look closely at the training you have accomplished and the results you have achieved for this season.

What are your strengths so far this season as an athlete?

What are your weaknesses so far this season as an athlete?

What's your most significant accomplishment so far this season?

Have you begun to think about offseason training? If so, what are your plans?

If you're on a team, respond to the following prompts:

This year our team strengths include...

This year our team weaknesses include...

Write about your best personal performance this season. What contributed to your success?

Write about your worst performance this season. What contributed to your weakness?

Training Priorities for the Season

Go back to the three Training Priorities that you established at the beginning of this workbook. List them below. Rank your effectiveness on each numeric chart:

Priority 1: _____

0——1——2——3——4——5——6——7——8——9——10

Poor   Average   Great

Priority 2: _____

0——1——2——3——4——5——6——7——8——9——10

Poor   Average   Great

Priority 3: _____

0——1——2——3——4——5——6——7——8——9——10

Poor   Average   Great

Personal Athletic Goals

Go back to the three Personal Athletic Goals that you established at the beginning of this workbook. List them below. Rank your effectiveness in each on the numeric chart.

Goal 1: _____

0——1——2——3——4——5——6——7——8——9——10

Poor   Average   Great

Goal 2: _____

0——1——2——3——4——5——6——7——8——9——10

Poor   Average   Great

Goal 3: _____

0——1——2——3——4——5——6——7——8——9——10

Poor   Average   Great

Midseason Thoughts (cont.)

Midseason Letter

Write a letter about your performance thus far to your coach, training partner, a fellow athlete... or to *yourself*.

Training Log #36

Date_____   Location_____

Hours of sleep: _____ Body weight: _____ Health: _____ Hydration: _____

Nutrition: Grains: _____ Veggies: _____ Fruits: _____ Protein: _____

Activities:

_____ Intensity Level: _____   Time: _____

_____ Intensity Level: _____   Time: _____

_____ Intensity Level: _____   Time: _____

_____ Intensity Level: _____   Time: _____

_____ Intensity Level: _____   Time: _____

_____ Intensity Level: _____   Time: _____

_____ Intensity Level: _____   Time: _____

Total Training Time: _____ Total Season Time: _____

Other activities: _____

Notes on Training:
_____
_____
_____

To-do Lists:

Sport: Studies/Work:

_____   _____

_____   _____

_____   _____

_____   _____

Today's Training Experience

Day 37 *Date*_____

Rapid Response

Write about the following topics:

Mental preparedness

Managing Anxiety or Nervousness

Motivation

Coping with Success

Handling Failure

Training Log #37

Date_____   Location_____

Hours of sleep: _____ Body weight: _____ Health: _____ Hydration: _____

Nutrition: Grains: _____Veggies: _____ Fruits: _____ Protein: _____

Activities:

_____ Intensity Level: _____   Time: _____

_____ Intensity Level: _____   Time: _____

_____ Intensity Level: _____   Time: _____

_____ Intensity Level: _____   Time: _____

_____ Intensity Level: _____   Time: _____

_____ Intensity Level: _____   Time: _____

_____ Intensity Level: _____   Time: _____

Total Training Time: _____ Total Season Time: _____

Other activities: _____

Notes on Training:
_____
_____
_____

To-do Lists:

Sport: Studies/Work:

_____   _____

_____   _____

_____   _____

_____   _____

Today's Training Experience

Day 38 Date_____

How Do You Learn?

How do you learn your sport? Look at this figure and circle the ways you learn as an athlete.

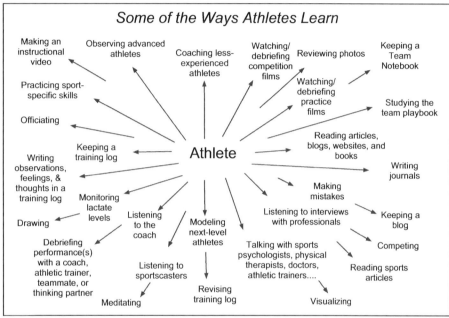

Reprinted with permission from Writing on the Bus *(Kent, 2011, p. 14)*

Looking at the various learning tools above, what could you add to your own training and learning experience to help you improve as an athlete?

Are there ways you learn that are not included in the figure above? List them below. (Please write to tell me: rich.kent@maine.edu):

Training Log #38

Date_____   Location_____

Hours of sleep: _____ Body weight: _____ Health: _____ Hydration: _____

Nutrition: Grains: _____Veggies: _____ Fruits: _____ Protein: _____

Activities:

_____ Intensity Level: _____   Time: _____

_____ Intensity Level: _____   Time: _____

_____ Intensity Level: _____   Time: _____

_____ Intensity Level: _____   Time: _____

_____ Intensity Level: _____   Time: _____

_____ Intensity Level: _____   Time: _____

_____ Intensity Level: _____   Time: _____

Total Training Time: _____ Total Season Time: _____

Other activities: _____

Notes on Training:

_____
_____
_____

To-do Lists:

Sport: Studies/Work:

_____   _____
_____   _____
_____   _____
_____   _____

Today's Training Experience

Day 39 *Date_____*

So far this season...

The funniest thing I've witnessed...

The happiest I've been...

The thing I thought but did not say to a coach, opponent, official, or teammate...

The moment I wish I could take back...

Training Log #39

Date_____   Location_____

Hours of sleep: _____ Body weight: _____ Health: _____ Hydration: _____

Nutrition: Grains: _____ Veggies: _____ Fruits: _____ Protein: _____

Activities:

_____ Intensity Level: _____   Time: _____

_____ Intensity Level: _____   Time: _____

_____ Intensity Level: _____   Time: _____

_____ Intensity Level: _____   Time: _____

_____ Intensity Level: _____   Time: _____

_____ Intensity Level: _____   Time: _____

_____ Intensity Level: _____   Time: _____

Total Training Time: _____ Total Season Time: _____

Other activities: _____

Notes on Training:

_____
_____
_____

To-do Lists:

Sport: Studies/Work:

_____   _____
_____   _____
_____   _____
_____   _____

☐   Today's Training Experience

Day 40 Date_____

Are you getting enough sleep?

"Sleep is food for the brain."
–The National Sleep Foundation

Go back through your workbook thus far and add up the total hours of sleep you've had. Divide the total hours of sleep by the number of days you kept track.

TOTAL HOURS OF SLEEP: _____ ÷ NUMBER OF DAYS_____ =

_____ AVERAGE NIGHTLY HOURS OF SLEEP

The National Sleep Foundation suggests that the average teenager needs 9 ¼ hours of sleep per night and the average child aged five to 12 need 10-11 hours of sleep. Add an athlete's lifestyle to the equation and the hours of sleep necessary go up.

Write about your sleeping habits:

Training Log #40

Date_____   Location_____

Hours of sleep: _____ Body weight: _____ Health: _____ Hydration: _____

Nutrition: Grains: _____Veggies: _____ Fruits: _____ Protein: _____

Activities:

_____ Intensity Level: _____   Time: _____

_____ Intensity Level: _____   Time: _____

_____ Intensity Level: _____   Time: _____

_____ Intensity Level: _____   Time: _____

_____ Intensity Level: _____   Time: _____

_____ Intensity Level: _____   Time: _____

_____ Intensity Level: _____   Time: _____

Total Training Time: _____ Total Season Time: _____

Other activities: _____

Notes on Training:

_____
_____
_____

To-do Lists:

Sport: Studies/Work:

_____   _____

_____   _____

_____   _____

_____   _____

Today's Training Experience

Day 41 Date_____

Competition Analysis II

Team/Athlete #1_____   Team/Athlete #2_____

Strengths: Strengths:

Weaknesses: Weaknesses:

Adjustments at the halfway point: Adjustments at the halfway point:

Comparisons: If you watched two football teams, compare their offenses and defenses, their quarterbacks, linesmen, and receivers. If you watched two tennis players, compare the players' service games, net points, or composure. If you watched a road race, select two favorite runners and discuss issues such as their strategies, stride, and fitness:

Describe the critical moment of the competition:

Final Analysis: Think as a coach about strengths and/or weaknesses (e.g., athleticism, speed, coaching, motivation/ heart). What adjustments might you have suggested to either team/athlete if you were the coach?

Training Log #41

Date_____   Location_____

Hours of sleep: _____ Body weight: _____ Health: _____ Hydration: _____

Nutrition: Grains: _____Veggies: _____ Fruits: _____ Protein: _____

Activities:

_____ Intensity Level: _____   Time: _____

_____ Intensity Level: _____   Time: _____

_____ Intensity Level: _____   Time: _____

_____ Intensity Level: _____   Time: _____

_____ Intensity Level: _____   Time: _____

_____ Intensity Level: _____   Time: _____

_____ Intensity Level: _____   Time: _____

Total Training Time: _____ Total Season Time: _____

Other activities: _____

Notes on Training:

_____
_____
_____

To-do Lists:

Sport: Studies/Work:

_____   _____

_____   _____

_____   _____

_____   _____

Today's Training Experience

Day 42 *Date*_____

Performance Analysis

(Designed by Sheila Stawinski of the University of Vermont.)

Complete this form just after a competition.

Opponent: _____ Date: _____

What were your stressors for this competition?

How did you experience the stress? (thoughts, feelings, actions)

How was your level of arousal for the competition? Mark on this scale:

0——————————————5——————————————10

Too Low   *Perfect*   *Too High*

List in a word or two what your feelings were at the various times in the day?

Travel to event: Warm up:

Just before the competition: During the competition:

What techniques did you use to manage the stress? How effective were you in controlling it?

How was your self-talk? Positive, negative, thoughtful? Explain:

What did you enjoy about the competition?

How would you rate your effort? 0——————5——————10

Poor   Average   Great

Additional Comments:

Training Log #42

Date_____   Location_____

Hours of sleep: _____ Body weight: _____ Health: _____ Hydration: _____

Nutrition: Grains: _____Veggies: _____ Fruits: _____ Protein: _____

Activities:

_____ Intensity Level: _____   Time: _____

_____ Intensity Level: _____   Time: _____

_____ Intensity Level: _____   Time: _____

_____ Intensity Level: _____   Time: _____

_____ Intensity Level: _____   Time: _____

_____ Intensity Level: _____   Time: _____

_____ Intensity Level: _____   Time: _____

Total Training Time: _____ Total Season Time: _____

Other activities: _____

Notes on Training:

_____
_____
_____

To-do Lists:

Sport: Studies/Work:

_____   _____

_____   _____

_____   _____

_____   _____

☐ Today's Training Experience

Day 43 Date_____

Your Most Humiliating Day as an Athlete

Swedish soccer player Jonathan Szeps wrote the following journal entry as a 17-year old high school exchange student:

I easily remember the most humiliating day as an athlete. It was about three years ago when my team had an away game in a suburb called Rinkeby. Rinkeby is one of the suburbs in Sweden with a lot of crimes and problems. It is also a suburb with a majority of immigrants. In my team, almost everybody has their roots in Sweden (I'm one of the few who doesn't). Everybody on the team also comes from pretty wealthy families. A lot of my teammates has a lot of prejudice of Rinkeby. Before the game everybody was joking about how we would get robbed after the game after we easily had defeated the team.

When we arrived to the field the win seemed even more obvious. The field was a joke. Not as big as it should have been in our age, not grass, no nets in the goal and the team we were playing didn't even wear the same cloths. We expected an easy victory but we were SO WRONG!

The team, called Benadir, gave us a lesson how to play soccer. On a shitty field in the middle of nowhere they played like the Brazilian national team. They played with us, making cool tricks and scoring beautiful goals. At the end of the first half the score was 10-0 and we couldn't believe what we just had experienced. After some yelling from our coach we got back out for second half. We played a little bit better, scoring two goals (I scored one) but we still got beat by 16-2. After the game, instead of robbing us, the players were really nice to us and behaved like a winner should. We were so embarrassed and all of us didn't say a word on way back home. This really proved us wrong about prejudices. I will never forget that loss.

What are your thoughts about Jonathan's experience? Have you had a similar experience?

Training Log #43

Date_____   Location_____

Hours of sleep: _____ Body weight: _____ Health: _____ Hydration: _____

Nutrition: Grains: _____Veggies: _____ Fruits: _____ Protein: _____

Activities:

_____ Intensity Level: _____   Time: _____

_____ Intensity Level: _____   Time: _____

_____ Intensity Level: _____   Time: _____

_____ Intensity Level: _____   Time: _____

_____ Intensity Level: _____   Time: _____

_____ Intensity Level: _____   Time: _____

_____ Intensity Level: _____   Time: _____

Total Training Time: _____ Total Season Time: _____

Other activities: _____

Notes on Training:
_____
_____
_____

To-do Lists:

Sport: Studies/Work:

_____   _____
_____   _____
_____   _____
_____   _____

Today's Training Experience

Day 44 *Date*_____

Stressed?

The American College of Sports Medicine listed the following signs and symptoms of stress in athletes.

Behavioral	Physical	Psychological
Difficulty sleeping	Feeling ill	Negative self-talk
Lack of focus, overwhelmed	Cold, clammy hands	Inability to concentrate
Consistently performs better in practice/training than in competition	Profuse sweating	Uncontrollable intrusive and negative thoughts or images
Substance abuse	Headaches	Self doubt
	Increased muscle tension	
	Altered appetite	

Referring to the chart above, write about your stress levels in each of the following areas:

Behavioral:

Physical:

Psychological:

Training Log #44

Date_____   Location_____

Hours of sleep: _____ Body weight: _____ Health: _____ Hydration: _____

Nutrition: Grains: _____Veggies: _____ Fruits: _____ Protein: _____

Activities:

_____ Intensity Level: _____   Time: _____

_____ Intensity Level: _____   Time: _____

_____ Intensity Level: _____   Time: _____

_____ Intensity Level: _____   Time: _____

_____ Intensity Level: _____   Time: _____

_____ Intensity Level: _____   Time: _____

_____ Intensity Level: _____   Time: _____

Total Training Time: _____ Total Season Time: _____

Other activities: _____

Notes on Training:
_____
_____
_____

To-do Lists:

Sport: Studies/Work:

_____   _____

_____   _____

_____   _____

_____   _____

Today's Training Experience

Day 45 *Date*_____

Halftime Talk

Using a recent competition, create the halftime or post-game talk that you would have given as the opponent's coach. Remember to include as many specifics as possible.

Training Log #45

Date_____   Location_____

Hours of sleep: _____ Body weight: _____ Health: _____ Hydration: _____

Nutrition: Grains: _____Veggies: _____ Fruits: _____ Protein: _____

Activities:

_____ Intensity Level: _____   Time: _____

_____ Intensity Level: _____   Time: _____

_____ Intensity Level: _____   Time: _____

_____ Intensity Level: _____   Time: _____

_____ Intensity Level: _____   Time: _____

_____ Intensity Level: _____   Time: _____

_____ Intensity Level: _____   Time: _____

Total Training Time: _____ Total Season Time: _____

Other activities: _____

Notes on Training:
_____
_____
_____

To-do Lists:

Sport: Studies/Work:

_____   _____

_____   _____

_____   _____

_____   _____

Today's Training Experience

Day 46 *Date*_____

What is a good opponent?

Training Log #46

Date_____   Location_____

Hours of sleep: _____ Body weight: _____ Health: _____ Hydration: _____

Nutrition: Grains: _____Veggies: _____ Fruits: _____ Protein: _____

Activities:

_____ Intensity Level: _____   Time: _____

_____ Intensity Level: _____   Time: _____

_____ Intensity Level: _____   Time: _____

_____ Intensity Level: _____   Time: _____

_____ Intensity Level: _____   Time: _____

_____ Intensity Level: _____   Time: _____

_____ Intensity Level: _____   Time: _____

Total Training Time: _____ Total Season Time: _____

Other activities: _____

Notes on Training:
_____
_____
_____

To-do Lists:

Sport: Studies/Work:

_____   _____

_____   _____

_____   _____

_____   _____

Today's Training Experience

Day 47 *Date*_____

Your Choice

Select one or more of the terms on the left and write:

Poor sport

Great eye

A good loss

Poser

Future pro

Injury

Suck-up

Cheat

Focus

Training

Fitness

Teammate

Official

Coach

Trainer

Foul

Frightened

Technical

Discipline

Reward

Practice

Training Log #47

Date_____   Location_____

Hours of sleep: _____ Body weight: _____ Health: _____ Hydration: _____

Nutrition: Grains: _____Veggies: _____ Fruits: _____ Protein: _____

Activities:

_____ Intensity Level: _____   Time: _____

_____ Intensity Level: _____   Time: _____

_____ Intensity Level: _____   Time: _____

_____ Intensity Level: _____   Time: _____

_____ Intensity Level: _____   Time: _____

_____ Intensity Level: _____   Time: _____

_____ Intensity Level: _____   Time: _____

Total Training Time: _____ Total Season Time: _____

Other activities: _____

Notes on Training:

_____
_____
_____

To-do Lists:

Sport: Studies/Work:

_____   _____

_____   _____

_____   _____

_____   _____

Today's Training Experience

Day 48 *Date*_____

Full Contact Poetry

Make a list of words that are common in your sport. In football you might include destiny, glory, ball, explosive, bronzed images, man, and love. Then, take those words and find creative ways to put them together. Checkout one example titled "Football."

FOOTBALL

Floating.
Hard motion.
Bronzed images of old.
A man. A ball.
Explosions of power
Like T.N.T.
Dancing, forgiving.
Coursing moves.
Expecting.
Destinies collide
And live to rise again.
Not for glory
For love.

by Scott Marchildon

Training Log #48

Date_____   Location_____

Hours of sleep: _____ Body weight: _____ Health: _____ Hydration: _____

Nutrition: Grains: _____Veggies: _____ Fruits: _____ Protein: _____

Activities:

_____ Intensity Level: _____   Time: _____

_____ Intensity Level: _____   Time: _____

_____ Intensity Level: _____   Time: _____

_____ Intensity Level: _____   Time: _____

_____ Intensity Level: _____   Time: _____

_____ Intensity Level: _____   Time: _____

_____ Intensity Level: _____   Time: _____

Total Training Time: _____ Total Season Time: _____

Other activities: _____

Notes on Training:
_____
_____
_____

To-do Lists:

Sport: Studies/Work:

_____   _____

_____   _____

_____   _____

_____   _____

Today's Training Experience

Day 49 Date_____

Letter to the Opposing Coach

Write a letter to an opposing coach. Here's was written in a journal by a soccer player:

> Dear Coach,
>
> You have a great team. They are disciplined and organized and the kids were good guys even though they kicked our butts! Your players had wicked good talk. They supported each other with talk. Our coach always tells us to play the way we are facing. At tonight's match I could see that. I was impressed how your midfielders used their defenders so well. They got out of a lot of trouble with quick back passes. I also thought your one and two touch passes were _useful_ as our coach says. We learned a lot today and I am proud of the way we played even though we lost 3-1. Some day I hope our team will play like yours. Good luck with the rest of your season.
>
> Sincerely,
>
> Kevin
> #11 Falcon Soccer

Training Log #49

Date_____   Location_____

Hours of sleep: _____ Body weight: _____ Health: _____ Hydration: _____

Nutrition: Grains: _____Veggies: _____ Fruits: _____ Protein: _____

Activities:

_____ Intensity Level: _____   Time: _____

_____ Intensity Level: _____   Time: _____

_____ Intensity Level: _____   Time: _____

_____ Intensity Level: _____   Time: _____

_____ Intensity Level: _____   Time: _____

_____ Intensity Level: _____   Time: _____

_____ Intensity Level: _____   Time: _____

Total Training Time: _____ Total Season Time: _____

Other activities: _____

Notes on Training:

_____
_____
_____

To-do Lists:

Sport: Studies/Work:

_____   _____
_____   _____
_____   _____
_____   _____

☐ Today's Training Experience

Day 50 *Date*_____

At This Moment...

You may be well into the competitive season. How do you feel about the following:

Training

Competitions

Coaching

Rest

Nutrition

Life beyond sport (e.g., family, school, work)

The rest of the season

What I need right now

Training Log #50

Date_____   Location_____

Hours of sleep: _____ Body weight: _____ Health: _____ Hydration: _____

Nutrition: Grains: _____Veggies: _____ Fruits: _____ Protein: _____

Activities:

_____ Intensity Level: _____   Time: _____

_____ Intensity Level: _____   Time: _____

_____ Intensity Level: _____   Time: _____

_____ Intensity Level: _____   Time: _____

_____ Intensity Level: _____   Time: _____

_____ Intensity Level: _____   Time: _____

_____ Intensity Level: _____   Time: _____

Total Training Time: _____ Total Season Time: _____

Other activities: _____

Notes on Training:

_____
_____
_____

To-do Lists:

Sport: Studies/Work:

_____   _____

_____   _____

_____   _____

_____   _____

☐ Today's Training Experience

Day 51 *Date_____*

Word Clouds

Go back to Day 50's journal entry and select individual words that reflect you and your season thus far. If you skipped Day 50, go back through your Training Logs and select words from "Notes on Training." Using a free online Word Cloud program like Wordle (www.wordle.net) or Tagxedo (www.tagxedo.com), create a word-art interpretation of your sports season so far. Print the Word Cloud, trim it with scissors, and tape it over the model supplied below. If you don't have access to Internet, sketch your own Word Cloud.

Training Log #51

Date_____   Location_____

Hours of sleep: _____ Body weight: _____ Health: _____ Hydration: _____

Nutrition: Grains: _____Veggies: _____ Fruits: _____ Protein: _____

Activities:

_____ Intensity Level: _____   Time: _____

_____ Intensity Level: _____   Time: _____

_____ Intensity Level: _____   Time: _____

_____ Intensity Level: _____   Time: _____

_____ Intensity Level: _____   Time: _____

_____ Intensity Level: _____   Time: _____

_____ Intensity Level: _____   Time: _____

Total Training Time: _____ Total Season Time: _____

Other activities: _____

Notes on Training:

_____
_____
_____

To-do Lists:

Sport: Studies/Work:

_____   _____

_____   _____

_____   _____

_____   _____

Today's Training Experience

Day 52 Date_____

What I think about...

What I think about during training:

What I think about during a competition:

What I think about after a win:

What I think about after a loss:

Training Log #52

Date_____   Location_____

Hours of sleep: _____ Body weight: _____ Health: _____ Hydration: _____

Nutrition: Grains: _____Veggies: _____ Fruits: _____ Protein: _____

Activities:

_____ Intensity Level: _____   Time: _____

_____ Intensity Level: _____   Time: _____

_____ Intensity Level: _____   Time: _____

_____ Intensity Level: _____   Time: _____

_____ Intensity Level: _____   Time: _____

_____ Intensity Level: _____   Time: _____

_____ Intensity Level: _____   Time: _____

Total Training Time: _____ Total Season Time: _____

Other activities: _____

Notes on Training:

_____
_____
_____

To-do Lists:

Sport: Studies/Work:

_____   _____
_____   _____
_____   _____
_____   _____

☐   Today's Training Experience

Day 53 *Date*_____

Unexpected

Draw a picture of yourself or your team after an unexpected performance (good or bad).

Training Log #53

Date_____   Location_____

Hours of sleep: _____ Body weight: _____ Health: _____ Hydration: _____

Nutrition: Grains: _____ Veggies: _____ Fruits: _____ Protein: _____

Activities:

_____ Intensity Level: _____   Time: _____

_____ Intensity Level: _____   Time: _____

_____ Intensity Level: _____   Time: _____

_____ Intensity Level: _____   Time: _____

_____ Intensity Level: _____   Time: _____

_____ Intensity Level: _____   Time: _____

_____ Intensity Level: _____   Time: _____

Total Training Time: _____ Total Season Time: _____

Other activities: _____

Notes on Training:
_____
_____
_____

To-do Lists:

Sport: Studies/Work:

_____   _____

_____   _____

_____   _____

_____   _____

Today's Training Experience

Day 54 *Date*_____

Songs of My Sport

Make a list of your favorite songs:

Which favorite songs would you play...

The night before a big competition:
Song title: _____

Training:
Song title: _____

During a competition:
Song title: _____

The morning of a competition:
Song title: _____

After an upset win:
Song title: _____

After a loss to an opponent I could have beaten:
Song title: _____

When the season ends:
Song title: _____

Others:
Song title: _____

Others:
Song title: _____

Training Log #54

Date_____ Location_____

Hours of sleep: _____ Body weight: _____ Health: _____ Hydration: _____

Nutrition: Grains: _____Veggies: _____ Fruits: _____ Protein: _____

Activities:

_____ Intensity Level: _____   Time: _____

_____ Intensity Level: _____   Time: _____

_____ Intensity Level: _____   Time: _____

_____ Intensity Level: _____   Time: _____

_____ Intensity Level: _____   Time: _____

_____ Intensity Level: _____   Time: _____

_____ Intensity Level: _____   Time: _____

Total Training Time: _____ Total Season Time: _____

Other activities: _____

Notes on Training:

_____
_____
_____

To-do Lists:

Sport: Studies/Work:

_____   _____

_____   _____

_____   _____

_____   _____

Today's Training Experience

Day 55 *Date_____*

Unpacking Your Training Days: Day_____ to Day _____

Select the previous two or three weeks of training and look closely at your results.

Number of training days _____   What's your total training time? _____

Average nightly hours of sleep: _____

Hydration Assessment: How many _____ (+) _____ (O) _____ (–)

How many training days were (+)_____ (O)_____ (–)_____

What have you done well during this training period?

What do you think you need to improve upon?

Go back and read "Notes on Training." Take a word or phrase from each Training Day and place them below:

Does this list tell you anything about your training?

Assess (√) this period of training: _____ (+)_____ (O) _____ (–)

Training Log #55

Date_____   Location_____

Hours of sleep: _____ Body weight: _____ Health: _____ Hydration: _____

Nutrition: Grains: _____Veggies: _____ Fruits: _____ Protein: _____

Activities:

_____ Intensity Level: _____   Time: _____

_____ Intensity Level: _____   Time: _____

_____ Intensity Level: _____   Time: _____

_____ Intensity Level: _____   Time: _____

_____ Intensity Level: _____   Time: _____

_____ Intensity Level: _____   Time: _____

_____ Intensity Level: _____   Time: _____

Total Training Time: _____ Total Season Time: _____

Other activities: _____

Notes on Training:

_____
_____
_____

To-do Lists:

Sport: Studies/Work:

_____   _____

_____   _____

_____   _____

_____   _____

Today's Training Experience

Day 56 *Date*_____

Being Sponsored

How would your life as an athlete change if you had a sponsor who paid you $100,000 per year plus all of your expenses?

What if that sponsor placed the following condition on your sponsorship: If you do not land in the top 10% in all of your competitions in Year One, we will cut your sponsorship by half ($50,000). In Year Two, if you do not perform in the top 10% in each competition, we will drop the sponsorship by another half ($25,000). By Year Three, if you're not performing consistently in the top 10%, you will be dropped.

Training Log #56

Date_____   Location_____

Hours of sleep: _____ Body weight: _____ Health: _____ Hydration: _____

Nutrition: Grains: _____Veggies: _____ Fruits: _____ Protein: _____

Activities:

_____ Intensity Level: _____   Time: _____

_____ Intensity Level: _____   Time: _____

_____ Intensity Level: _____   Time: _____

_____ Intensity Level: _____   Time: _____

_____ Intensity Level: _____   Time: _____

_____ Intensity Level: _____   Time: _____

_____ Intensity Level: _____   Time: _____

Total Training Time: _____ Total Season Time: _____

Other activities: _____

Notes on Training:
_____
_____
_____

To-do Lists:

Sport: Studies/Work:

_____   _____
_____   _____
_____   _____
_____   _____

☐ Today's Training Experience

Day 57 *Date*_____

Competition Analysis II

Team/Athlete #1_____   Team/Athlete #2_____

Strengths: Strengths:

Weaknesses: Weaknesses:

Adjustments at the halfway point: Adjustments at the halfway point:

Comparisons: If you watched two football teams, compare their offenses and defenses, their quarterbacks, linesmen, and receivers. If you watched two tennis players, compare the players' service games, net points, or composure. If you watched a road race, select two favorite runners and discuss issues such as their strategies, stride, and fitness:

Describe the critical moment of the competition:

Final Analysis: Think as a coach about strengths and/or weaknesses (e.g., athleticism, speed, coaching, motivation/ heart). What adjustments might you have suggested to either team/athlete if you were the coach?

Training Log #57

Date_____   Location_____

Hours of sleep: _____ Body weight: _____ Health: _____ Hydration: _____

Nutrition: Grains: _____Veggies: _____ Fruits: _____ Protein: _____

Activities:

_____ Intensity Level: _____   Time: _____

_____ Intensity Level: _____   Time: _____

_____ Intensity Level: _____   Time: _____

_____ Intensity Level: _____   Time: _____

_____ Intensity Level: _____   Time: _____

_____ Intensity Level: _____   Time: _____

_____ Intensity Level: _____   Time: _____

Total Training Time: _____ Total Season Time: _____

Other activities: _____

Notes on Training:

_____
_____
_____

To-do Lists:

Sport: Studies/Work:

_____   _____

_____   _____

_____   _____

_____   _____

Today's Training Experience

Day 58 *Date_____*

Your Thoughtful Side

Tell about the kindest thing you have ever done as an athlete.

Training Log #58

Date_____   Location_____

Hours of sleep: _____ Body weight: _____ Health: _____ Hydration: _____

Nutrition: Grains: _____Veggies: _____ Fruits: _____ Protein: _____

Activities:

_____ Intensity Level: _____   Time: _____

_____ Intensity Level: _____   Time: _____

_____ Intensity Level: _____   Time: _____

_____ Intensity Level: _____   Time: _____

_____ Intensity Level: _____   Time: _____

_____ Intensity Level: _____   Time: _____

_____ Intensity Level: _____   Time: _____

Total Training Time: _____ Total Season Time: _____

Other activities: _____

Notes on Training:
_____
_____
_____

To-do Lists:

Sport: Studies/Work:

_____   _____

_____   _____

_____   _____

_____   _____

Today's Training Experience

Day 59 *Date*_____

World-Class Thoughts

Now that you've had experience writing in an athlete's journal, look back through the journal themes of the same 30-year-old world-class athlete:

Loneliness	Relaxation	Lists
Training	Breathing	Equipment
Family	Preparation	Sponsors
Friends	Control	Balance
Focus	Routine	Alignment
Emotions	Yoga	Symmetry
Food	Writing	Asserting
Dreams	Need for	oneself
Body Tension	success	Satisfaction
Colors	Self-esteem	Optimism
Visualization	Playfulness	Goals
Awareness	Schedules	

How do you view this elite athlete's list now that you have an increased experience as an athlete who writes?

What additional themes have you written about this season?

Training Log #59

Date_____   Location_____

Hours of sleep: _____ Body weight: _____ Health: _____ Hydration: _____

Nutrition: Grains: _____Veggies: _____ Fruits: _____ Protein: _____

Activities:

_____ Intensity Level: _____   Time: _____

_____ Intensity Level: _____   Time: _____

_____ Intensity Level: _____   Time: _____

_____ Intensity Level: _____   Time: _____

_____ Intensity Level: _____   Time: _____

_____ Intensity Level: _____   Time: _____

_____ Intensity Level: _____   Time: _____

Total Training Time: _____ Total Season Time: _____

Other activities: _____

Notes on Training:

_____
_____
_____

To-do Lists:

Sport: Studies/Work:

_____   _____

_____   _____

_____   _____

_____   _____

Today's Training Experience

Day 60 *Date*_____

Equipment

Draw a picture of your favorite piece of sports equipment (e.g., baseball glove, football cleats, lacrosse stick). Write a title and a caption for your drawing.

Training Log #60

Date_____   Location_____

Hours of sleep: _____ Body weight: _____ Health: _____ Hydration: _____

Nutrition: Grains: _____Veggies: _____ Fruits: _____ Protein: _____

Activities:

_____ Intensity Level: _____   Time: _____

_____ Intensity Level: _____   Time: _____

_____ Intensity Level: _____   Time: _____

_____ Intensity Level: _____   Time: _____

_____ Intensity Level: _____   Time: _____

_____ Intensity Level: _____   Time: _____

_____ Intensity Level: _____   Time: _____

Total Training Time: _____ Total Season Time: _____

Other activities: _____

Notes on Training:
_____
_____
_____

To-do Lists:

Sport: Studies/Work:

_____   _____

_____   _____

_____   _____

_____   _____

Today's Training Experience

Day 61 *Date*_____

Props

What special story would you like told about a teammate, coach, fan, or opponent and why?

Training Log #61

Date_____   Location_____

Hours of sleep: _____ Body weight: _____ Health: _____ Hydration: _____

Nutrition: Grains: _____Veggies: _____ Fruits: _____ Protein: _____

Activities:

_____ Intensity Level: _____   Time: _____

_____ Intensity Level: _____   Time: _____

_____ Intensity Level: _____   Time: _____

_____ Intensity Level: _____   Time: _____

_____ Intensity Level: _____   Time: _____

_____ Intensity Level: _____   Time: _____

_____ Intensity Level: _____   Time: _____

Total Training Time: _____ Total Season Time: _____

Other activities: _____

Notes on Training:

_____
_____
_____

To-do Lists:

Sport: Studies/Work:

_____   _____

_____   _____

_____   _____

_____   _____

☐   Today's Training Experience

Day 62 *Date*_____

Now

Write from the perspective of your youngest competitive self about the athlete you have become.

Training Log #62

Date_____   Location_____

Hours of sleep: _____ Body weight: _____ Health: _____ Hydration: _____

Nutrition: Grains: _____Veggies: _____ Fruits: _____ Protein: _____

Activities:

_____ Intensity Level: _____   Time: _____

_____ Intensity Level: _____   Time: _____

_____ Intensity Level: _____   Time: _____

_____ Intensity Level: _____   Time: _____

_____ Intensity Level: _____   Time: _____

_____ Intensity Level: _____   Time: _____

_____ Intensity Level: _____   Time: _____

Total Training Time: _____ Total Season Time: _____

Other activities: _____

Notes on Training:

_____
_____
_____

To-do Lists:

Sport: Studies/Work:

_____   _____

_____   _____

_____   _____

_____   _____

☐   Today's Training Experience

Day 63 *Date*_____

Three-Week Analysis

Using the *above average* (+), *average* (O), and *below average* (–) ratings from the past three weeks, draw three line graphs for your health, hydration, and training experiences. What do these graphs tell you? Here's a model of 21 days of Training Experiences taken from the box at the bottom of each Training Log:

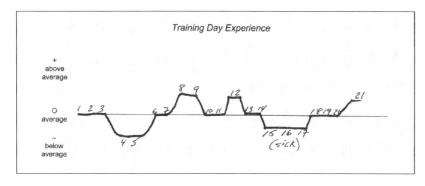

Hydration

+

0 ~~~~~~

–

Health

+

0 ~~~~~~

–

Training

+

0 ~~~~~~

–

Training Log #63

Date_____   Location_____

Hours of sleep: _____ Body weight: _____ Health: _____ Hydration: _____

Nutrition: Grains: _____Veggies: _____ Fruits: _____ Protein: _____

Activities:

_____ Intensity Level: _____   Time: _____

_____ Intensity Level: _____   Time: _____

_____ Intensity Level: _____   Time: _____

_____ Intensity Level: _____   Time: _____

_____ Intensity Level: _____   Time: _____

_____ Intensity Level: _____   Time: _____

_____ Intensity Level: _____   Time: _____

Total Training Time: _____ Total Season Time: _____

Other activities: _____

Notes on Training:

_____
_____
_____

To-do Lists:

Sport: Studies/Work:

_____   _____

_____   _____

_____   _____

_____   _____

Today's Training Experience

Day 64 *Date*_____

Practicing to the Next Level?

Write about a recent practice session. What could you have done differently to move toward the next level?

Training Log #64

Date_____   Location_____

Hours of sleep: _____ Body weight: _____ Health: _____ Hydration: _____

Nutrition: Grains: _____Veggies: _____ Fruits: _____ Protein: _____

Activities:

_____ Intensity Level: _____   Time: _____

_____ Intensity Level: _____   Time: _____

_____ Intensity Level: _____   Time: _____

_____ Intensity Level: _____   Time: _____

_____ Intensity Level: _____   Time: _____

_____ Intensity Level: _____   Time: _____

_____ Intensity Level: _____   Time: _____

Total Training Time: _____ Total Season Time: _____

Other activities: _____

Notes on Training:
_____
_____
_____

To-do Lists:

Sport: Studies/Work:

_____   _____

_____   _____

_____   _____

_____   _____

Today's Training Experience

Day 65 *Date*_____

This Season

What are you going to miss about this season?

Training Log #65

Date_____   Location_____

Hours of sleep: _____ Body weight: _____ Health: _____ Hydration: _____

Nutrition: Grains: _____Veggies: _____ Fruits: _____ Protein: _____

Activities:

_____ Intensity Level: _____   Time: _____

_____ Intensity Level: _____   Time: _____

_____ Intensity Level: _____   Time: _____

_____ Intensity Level: _____   Time: _____

_____ Intensity Level: _____   Time: _____

_____ Intensity Level: _____   Time: _____

_____ Intensity Level: _____   Time: _____

Total Training Time: _____ Total Season Time: _____

Other activities: _____

Notes on Training:

_____
_____
_____

To-do Lists:

Sport: Studies/Work:

_____   _____

_____   _____

_____   _____

_____   _____

[ ]   Today's Training Experience

Day 66 *Date*_____

People of My Sport

Throughout your career as an athlete, you have encountered many types of people. Tell the stories of the following and what you've learned by thinking about their behaviors:

The obnoxious fan   The kind-hearted coach

The _____ official   The competitor you immediately liked.

Training Log #66

Date_____   Location_____

Hours of sleep: _____ Body weight: _____ Health: _____ Hydration: _____

Nutrition: Grains: _____Veggies: _____ Fruits: _____ Protein: _____

Activities:

_____ Intensity Level: _____   Time: _____

_____ Intensity Level: _____   Time: _____

_____ Intensity Level: _____   Time: _____

_____ Intensity Level: _____   Time: _____

_____ Intensity Level: _____   Time: _____

_____ Intensity Level: _____   Time: _____

_____ Intensity Level: _____   Time: _____

Total Training Time: _____ Total Season Time: _____

Other activities: _____

Notes on Training:
_____
_____
_____

To-do Lists:

Sport: Studies/Work:

_____   _____

_____   _____

_____   _____

_____   _____

Today's Training Experience

Day 67 *Date_____*

Numbers Game: The Season's Stats

Come up with as many statistics as possible from your competitive season. These stats may be serious and not so serious. Here are a few ideas to jumpstart your list—you may want to use one of the Notes Pages at the back of your workbook:

-How many training hours?

-Number of miles traveled to competitions?

-How many competitions?

-How many hours/miles run?

-Stats about scores, times, wins, losses.

-How many sports t-shirts did you receive?

-How many hours lifting weights?

How many bananas eaten?

-How often did you stop at fast-food place after a competition or practice?

More:

_____

_____

_____

_____

_____

_____

Training Log #67

Date_____   Location_____

Hours of sleep: _____ Body weight: _____ Health: _____ Hydration: _____

Nutrition: Grains: _____Veggies: _____ Fruits: _____ Protein: _____

Activities:

_____ Intensity Level: _____   Time: _____

_____ Intensity Level: _____   Time: _____

_____ Intensity Level: _____   Time: _____

_____ Intensity Level: _____   Time: _____

_____ Intensity Level: _____   Time: _____

_____ Intensity Level: _____   Time: _____

_____ Intensity Level: _____   Time: _____

Total Training Time: _____ Total Season Time: _____

Other activities: _____

Notes on Training:
_____
_____
_____

To-do Lists:

Sport: Studies/Work:

_____   _____

_____   _____

_____   _____

_____   _____

☐ Today's Training Experience

A Letter

Write a letter about your training and sports season to someone who cares for you.

Training Log #68

Date_____   Location_____

Hours of sleep: _____ Body weight: _____ Health: _____ Hydration: _____

Nutrition: Grains: _____Veggies: _____ Fruits: _____ Protein: _____

Activities:

_____ Intensity Level: _____   Time: _____

_____ Intensity Level: _____   Time: _____

_____ Intensity Level: _____   Time: _____

_____ Intensity Level: _____   Time: _____

_____ Intensity Level: _____   Time: _____

_____ Intensity Level: _____   Time: _____

_____ Intensity Level: _____   Time: _____

Total Training Time: _____ Total Season Time: _____

Other activities: _____

Notes on Training:
_____
_____
_____

To-do Lists:

Sport: Studies/Work:

_____   _____

_____   _____

_____   _____

_____   _____

☐   Today's Training Experience

Day 69 *Date*_____

For Another

Write about a time this season when you were genuinely happy for another athlete's success.

Training Log #69

Date_____   Location_____

Hours of sleep: _____ Body weight: _____ Health: _____ Hydration: _____

Nutrition: Grains: _____Veggies: _____ Fruits: _____ Protein: _____

Activities:

_____ Intensity Level: _____   Time: _____

_____ Intensity Level: _____   Time: _____

_____ Intensity Level: _____   Time: _____

_____ Intensity Level: _____   Time: _____

_____ Intensity Level: _____   Time: _____

_____ Intensity Level: _____   Time: _____

_____ Intensity Level: _____   Time: _____

Total Training Time: _____ Total Season Time: _____

Other activities: _____

Notes on Training:

_____
_____
_____

To-do Lists:

Sport: Studies/Work:

_____   _____

_____   _____

_____   _____

_____   _____

Today's Training Experience

Day 70 *Date*_____

Moments of the Season

Throughout athletic seasons you experience highs and lows, ups and down. Think back through the season and give quick examples of the following:

I laughed...

I cried or got emotional...

I screamed like a wild person...

I got crazy angry...

I sat and stared in disbelief...

I just didn't care...

I wanted to go hide...

I wanted someone to see...

Training Log #70

Date_____   Location_____

Hours of sleep: _____ Body weight: _____ Health: _____ Hydration: _____

Nutrition: Grains: _____Veggies: _____ Fruits: _____ Protein: _____

Activities:

_____ Intensity Level: _____   Time: _____

_____ Intensity Level: _____   Time: _____

_____ Intensity Level: _____   Time: _____

_____ Intensity Level: _____   Time: _____

_____ Intensity Level: _____   Time: _____

_____ Intensity Level: _____   Time: _____

_____ Intensity Level: _____   Time: _____

Total Training Time: _____ Total Season Time: _____

Other activities: _____

Notes on Training:
_____
_____
_____

To-do Lists:

Sport: Studies/Work:

_____   _____

_____   _____

_____   _____

_____   _____

Today's Training Experience

Day 71 *Date*_____

Your Sports Season

Think about your sports season and draw whatever comes to mind.

Training Log #71

Date_____   Location_____

Hours of sleep: _____ Body weight: _____ Health: _____ Hydration: _____

Nutrition: Grains: _____Veggies: _____ Fruits: _____ Protein: _____

Activities:

_____ Intensity Level: _____   Time: _____

_____ Intensity Level: _____   Time: _____

_____ Intensity Level: _____   Time: _____

_____ Intensity Level: _____   Time: _____

_____ Intensity Level: _____   Time: _____

_____ Intensity Level: _____   Time: _____

_____ Intensity Level: _____   Time: _____

Total Training Time: _____ Total Season Time: _____

Other activities: _____

Notes on Training:
_____
_____
_____

To-do Lists:

Sport: Studies/Work:

_____   _____

_____   _____

_____   _____

_____   _____

Today's Training Experience

Day 72 *Date*_____

Postseason Thoughts
Looking back to think forward

The prompts below will guide you in thinking back through your sports season. You'll also have an opportunity to look closely at the training you have accomplished and the results you have achieved this season.

What have been your strengths this season as an athlete?

What have been your weaknesses?

What's been your most significant accomplishment this season?

What are your plans for offseason training?

If you're on a team, respond to the following prompts:

      This year our team strengths include...

      This year our team weaknesses include...

Write about your best personal performance this season. What contributed to your success?

Write about your worst performance this season. What contributed to this performance?

Training Priorities for the Season

Go back to the three Training Priorities that you established at the beginning of this workbook. List and rank your effectiveness below.

Priority 1: _____

0—1—2—3—4—5—6—7—8—9—10
Poor   Average   Great

Priority 2: _____

0—1—2—3—4—5—6—7—8—9—10
Poor   Average   Great

Priority 3: _____

0—1—2—3—4—5—6—7—8—9—10
Poor   Average   Great

Personal Athletic Goals

Go back to the three Personal Athletic Goals that you established at the beginning of this workbook. List and rank your effectiveness below.

Goal 1: _____

0—1—2—3—4—5—6—7—8—9—10
Poor   Average   Great

Goal 2: _____

0—1—2—3—4—5—6—7—8—9—10
Poor   Average   Great

Goal 3: _____

0—1—2—3—4—5—6—7—8—9—10
Poor   Average   Great

Training Log #72

Date_____   Location_____

Hours of sleep: _____ Body weight: _____ Health: _____ Hydration: _____

Nutrition: Grains: _____Veggies: _____ Fruits: _____ Protein: _____

Activities:

_____ Intensity Level: _____   Time: _____

_____ Intensity Level: _____   Time: _____

_____ Intensity Level: _____   Time: _____

_____ Intensity Level: _____   Time: _____

_____ Intensity Level: _____   Time: _____

_____ Intensity Level: _____   Time: _____

_____ Intensity Level: _____   Time: _____

Total Training Time: _____ Total Season Time: _____

Other activities:
_____

Notes on Training:
_____
_____
_____

To-do Lists:

Sport: Studies/Work:

_____   _____

_____   _____

_____   _____

_____   _____

☐   Today's Training Experience

Competition Analysis I

Model Competition Analysis I for Team Athlete (Soccer)

Falcon Soccer
Match Analysis I

Falcons v. Leavitt Date: 9/17   Place: Away   Final: 1-0 Win
Records: Falcons: 4...W 0...L 0...D   Opponent: 3...W 1...L 0...D

- ✓ My strengths as a player in today's match: *Maintained defense's compactness. Right amount of talk—I didn't talk too much like at Lisbon. I had a* <u>*brilliant*</u> *run through the midfield into the attacking third...* ☺

- ✓ My weaknesses as a player in today's match: *I could have been more supportive of Jason. When I encourage him he plays better.*

- ✓ Team strengths in today's match: *We worked as a team—great support—positive comments... Good halftime adjustments.*

- ✓ Team weaknesses in today's match: *We could have been more inventive in attack during the 2nd half. We used Matt too much.*

- ✓ Opponent's strengths: *They never let down. #9 had warp-speed. His runs opened space and chances on goal.*

- ✓ Opponent's weaknesses: *Their midfielders and forwards did not mark us well in attack.*

- ✓ What was the "difference" in today's match: *Our midfielders support of the forwards...and, did I mention, a brilliant run by the sweeper?*

- ✓ What team adjustment would you suggest for the next match against this opponent? *#9=FAST. Move Dusty? More variety in attack.*

- ✓ Other comments about team strategy, attitude, preparation....
  We were prepared! The seniors had us ready to play.
               Un-DE-feated!

Model Competition Analysis I for Individual Athlete
(10k Road Racer)

Date: July 18   Opponent/Competition: *Swift River 10k Road Race*

Place: *Rumford*   Result: *36:47*

- My strengths as an athlete in the competition:
  I tapered my training for the 4 days before this race and felt great on race day. I ran with Tyler who has a better 10k time than me. I pushed myself. Good rest the night before.

- My weaknesses as an athlete in the competition:
  I think I could have pushed just a little bit more in the last kilometer—I had a little more energy left.

- Team strengths in the competition: *N/A*   Team weaknesses in the competition: *N/A*

- Opponent's strengths:
  Tyler: He congratulated me at the end of the race...
  Jason: he looked well stretched—really flexible —his stride was long and his pace was fantastic.

- Opponent's weaknesses:
  Jason: none today!
  Tyler: he kind of died on the final hill. I think he thought too much about me running behind him and he pushed too hard.

- What do you believe was the "difference" in the competition? What helped you do well or what seemed to hinder your performance today?
  Today, I ran well for the youngest in my age group. I know I'll get better as I get older and put in more miles.

- What adjustments might you make for your next competition?
  I will be more aware of the final kilometer to make sure that I use up everything.

- Other comments about strategy, attitude, and preparation.
  This race gave me confidence. I need to repeat my tapering plan for August 2 10k. Tagging on to Tyler worked... Maybe I should try staying with Jason? I need to talk to coach about that.

Competition Analysis I

Date: _____ Opponent/Competition: _____

Place: _____ Result: _____

- My strengths as an athlete in the competition:

- My weaknesses as an athlete in the competition:

- Team strengths in the competition:

- Team weaknesses in the competition:

- Opponent's strengths:

- Opponent's weaknesses:

- What do you believe was the "difference" in the competition? What helped you do well or what seemed to hinder your performance today?

- What adjustments might you make for your next competition?

- Other comments about strategy, attitude, and preparation.

Competition Analysis I

Date: _____   Opponent/Competition: _____

Place: _____   Result: _____

- My strengths as an athlete in the competition:

- My weaknesses as an athlete in the competition:

- Team strengths in the competition:

- Team weaknesses in the competition:

- Opponent's strengths:

- Opponent's weaknesses:

- What do you believe was the "difference" in the competition? What helped you do well or what seemed to hinder your performance today?

- What adjustments might you make for your next competition?

- Other comments about strategy, attitude, and preparation.

Competition Analysis I

Date: _____ Opponent/Competition: _____

Place: _____ Result: _____

- My strengths as an athlete in the competition:

- My weaknesses as an athlete in the competition:

- Team strengths in the competition:

- Team weaknesses in the competition:

- Opponent's strengths:

- Opponent's weaknesses:

- What do you believe was the "difference" in the competition? What helped you do well or what seemed to hinder your performance today?

- What adjustments might you make for your next competition?

- Other comments about strategy, attitude, and preparation.

Competition Analysis I

Date: _____   Opponent/Competition: _____

Place: _____   Result: _____

- My strengths as an athlete in the competition:

- My weaknesses as an athlete in the competition:

- Team strengths in the competition:

- Team weaknesses in the competition:

- Opponent's strengths:

- Opponent's weaknesses:

- What do you believe was the "difference" in the competition? What helped you do well or what seemed to hinder your performance today?

- What adjustments might you make for your next competition?

- Other comments about strategy, attitude, and preparation.

Competition Analysis I

Date: _____ Opponent/Competition: _____

Place: _____ Result: _____

- My strengths as an athlete in the competition:

- My weaknesses as an athlete in the competition:

- Team strengths in the competition:

- Team weaknesses in the competition:

- Opponent's strengths:

- Opponent's weaknesses:

- What do you believe was the "difference" in the competition? What helped you do well or what seemed to hinder your performance today?

- What adjustments might you make for your next competition?

- Other comments about strategy, attitude, and preparation.

Competition Analysis I

Date: _____   Opponent/Competition: _____

Place: _____   Result: _____

- My strengths as an athlete in the competition:

- My weaknesses as an athlete in the competition:

- Team strengths in the competition:

- Team weaknesses in the competition:

- Opponent's strengths:

- Opponent's weaknesses:

- What do you believe was the "difference" in the competition? What helped you do well or what seemed to hinder your performance today?

- What adjustments might you make for your next competition?

- Other comments about strategy, attitude, and preparation.

Competition Analysis I

Date: _____ Opponent/Competition: _____

Place: _____ Result: _____

- My strengths as an athlete in the competition:

- My weaknesses as an athlete in the competition:

- Team strengths in the competition:

- Team weaknesses in the competition:

- Opponent's strengths:

- Opponent's weaknesses:

- What do you believe was the "difference" in the competition? What helped you do well or what seemed to hinder your performance today?

- What adjustments might you make for your next competition?

- Other comments about strategy, attitude, and preparation.

Competition Analysis I

Date: _____   Opponent/Competition: _____

Place: _____   Result: _____

- My strengths as an athlete in the competition:

- My weaknesses as an athlete in the competition:

- Team strengths in the competition:

- Team weaknesses in the competition:

- Opponent's strengths:

- Opponent's weaknesses:

- What do you believe was the "difference" in the competition? What helped you do well or what seemed to hinder your performance today?

- What adjustments might you make for your next competition?

- Other comments about strategy, attitude, and preparation.

Competition Analysis I

Date: _____ Opponent/Competition: _____

Place: _____ Result: _____

- My strengths as an athlete in the competition:

- My weaknesses as an athlete in the competition:

- Team strengths in the competition:

- Team weaknesses in the competition:

- Opponent's strengths:

- Opponent's weaknesses:

- What do you believe was the "difference" in the competition? What helped you do well or what seemed to hinder your performance today?

- What adjustments might you make for your next competition?

- Other comments about strategy, attitude, and preparation.

Competition Analysis I

Date: _____   Opponent/Competition: _____

Place: _____   Result: _____

- My strengths as an athlete in the competition:

- My weaknesses as an athlete in the competition:

- Team strengths in the competition:

- Team weaknesses in the competition:

- Opponent's strengths:

- Opponent's weaknesses:

- What do you believe was the "difference" in the competition? What helped you do well or what seemed to hinder your performance today?

- What adjustments might you make for your next competition?

- Other comments about strategy, attitude, and preparation.

Competition Analysis I

Date: _____ Opponent/Competition: _____

Place: _____ Result: _____

- My strengths as an athlete in the competition:

- My weaknesses as an athlete in the competition:

- Team strengths in the competition:

- Team weaknesses in the competition:

- Opponent's strengths:

- Opponent's weaknesses:

- What do you believe was the "difference" in the competition? What helped you do well or what seemed to hinder your performance today?

- What adjustments might you make for your next competition?

- Other comments about strategy, attitude, and preparation.

Competition Analysis I

Date: _____   Opponent/Competition: _____

Place: _____   Result: _____

- My strengths as an athlete in the competition:

- My weaknesses as an athlete in the competition:

- Team strengths in the competition:

- Team weaknesses in the competition:

- Opponent's strengths:

- Opponent's weaknesses:

- What do you believe was the "difference" in the competition? What helped you do well or what seemed to hinder your performance today?

- What adjustments might you make for your next competition?

- Other comments about strategy, attitude, and preparation.

Competition Analysis I

Date: _____ Opponent/Competition: _____

Place: _____ Result: _____

- My strengths as an athlete in the competition:

- My weaknesses as an athlete in the competition:

- Team strengths in the competition:

- Team weaknesses in the competition:

- Opponent's strengths:

- Opponent's weaknesses:

- What do you believe was the "difference" in the competition? What helped you do well or what seemed to hinder your performance today?

- What adjustments might you make for your next competition?

- Other comments about strategy, attitude, and preparation.

Competition Analysis I

Date: _____   Opponent/Competition: _____

Place: _____   Result: _____

- My strengths as an athlete in the competition:

- My weaknesses as an athlete in the competition:

- Team strengths in the competition:

- Team weaknesses in the competition:

- Opponent's strengths:

- Opponent's weaknesses:

- What do you believe was the "difference" in the competition? What helped you do well or what seemed to hinder your performance today?

- What adjustments might you make for your next competition?

- Other comments about strategy, attitude, and preparation.

Competition Analysis I

Date: _____ Opponent/Competition: _____

Place: _____ Result: _____

- My strengths as an athlete in the competition:

- My weaknesses as an athlete in the competition:

- Team strengths in the competition:

- Team weaknesses in the competition:

- Opponent's strengths:

- Opponent's weaknesses:

- What do you believe was the "difference" in the competition? What helped you do well or what seemed to hinder your performance today?

- What adjustments might you make for your next competition?

- Other comments about strategy, attitude, and preparation.

Competition Analysis I

Date: _____   Opponent/Competition: _____

Place: _____   Result: _____

- My strengths as an athlete in the competition:

- My weaknesses as an athlete in the competition:

- Team strengths in the competition:

- Team weaknesses in the competition:

- Opponent's strengths:

- Opponent's weaknesses:

- What do you believe was the "difference" in the competition? What helped you do well or what seemed to hinder your performance today?

- What adjustments might you make for your next competition?

- Other comments about strategy, attitude, and preparation.

Competition Analysis I

Date: _____ Opponent/Competition: _____

Place: _____ Result: _____

– My strengths as an athlete in the competition:

– My weaknesses as an athlete in the competition:

– Team strengths in the competition:

– Team weaknesses in the competition:

– Opponent's strengths:

– Opponent's weaknesses:

– What do you believe was the "difference" in the competition? What helped you do well or what seemed to hinder your performance today?

– What adjustments might you make for your next competition?

– Other comments about strategy, attitude, and preparation.

Competition Analysis I

Date: _____   Opponent/Competition: _____

Place: _____   Result: _____

- My strengths as an athlete in the competition:

- My weaknesses as an athlete in the competition:

- Team strengths in the competition:

- Team weaknesses in the competition:

- Opponent's strengths:

- Opponent's weaknesses:

- What do you believe was the "difference" in the competition? What helped you do well or what seemed to hinder your performance today?

- What adjustments might you make for your next competition?

- Other comments about strategy, attitude, and preparation.

Competition Analysis I

Date: _____ Opponent/Competition: _____

Place: _____ Result: _____

- My strengths as an athlete in the competition:

- My weaknesses as an athlete in the competition:

- Team strengths in the competition:

- Team weaknesses in the competition:

- Opponent's strengths:

- Opponent's weaknesses:

- What do you believe was the "difference" in the competition? What helped you do well or what seemed to hinder your performance today?

- What adjustments might you make for your next competition?

- Other comments about strategy, attitude, and preparation.

Competition Analysis I

Date: _____ Opponent/Competition: _____

Place: _____ Result: _____

- My strengths as an athlete in the competition:

- My weaknesses as an athlete in the competition:

- Team strengths in the competition:

- Team weaknesses in the competition:

- Opponent's strengths:

- Opponent's weaknesses:

- What do you believe was the "difference" in the competition? What helped you do well or what seemed to hinder your performance today?

- What adjustments might you make for your next competition?

- Other comments about strategy, attitude, and preparation.

Injury Rehabilitation Plans

Model Injury Rehabilitation Plan

Injury Date: *Tuesday, July 18*   Trainer: *Aaron P.*

Diagnosis: *moderate ankle sprain*

Projected Timeline to Recovery: *7-10 days?*

Rehabilitation Plan:

Tuesday: RICE (Rest, Ice, Compression and Elevation). ACE bandage. Keep elevated. Check with parents about using anti-inflammatory medications for pain relief. Wednesday: keep elevated during school. See me in the afternoon.

Training Plan while Injured:

Wednesday: depending on severity ...weight room and swimming pool. Ice therapy w/ me. Thursday: RICE, keep elevated in school, see me... pool? Friday: keep elevated, RICE, see me, pool. Saturday: TBA...see me on Friday Sunday: TBA

What can you do to improve an aspect of your play while rehabilitating?

Swimming for upper body. Watch game videos. Stay connected with teammates.

What can you do for your teammates and coaches while rehabilitating?

> *–Don't whine about the injury.*
> *–Stay positive about recovery.*

Other thoughts:

Stay in the game!

*Adapted from Temple University Lacrosse

Injury Rehabilitation Plan

Injury Date:

Diagnosis:

Projected Timeline to Recovery:

Rehabilitation Plan:

Training Plan while Injured:

What can you do to improve an aspect of your play while rehabilitating?

What can you do for your teammates and coaches while rehabilitating?

Other thoughts:

Injury Rehabilitation Plan

Injury Date:

Diagnosis:

Projected Timeline to Recovery:

Rehabilitation Plan:

Training Plan while Injured:

What can you do to improve an aspect of your play while rehabilitating?

What can you do for your teammates and coaches while rehabilitating?

Other thoughts:

Injury Rehabilitation Plan

Injury Date:

Diagnosis:

Projected Timeline to Recovery:

Rehabilitation Plan:

Training Plan while Injured:

What can you do to improve an aspect of your play while rehabilitating?

What can you do for your teammates and coaches while rehabilitating?

Other thoughts:

Injury Rehabilitation Plan

Injury Date:

Diagnosis:

Projected Timeline to Recovery:

Rehabilitation Plan:

Training Plan while Injured:

What can you do to improve an aspect of your play while rehabilitating?

What can you do for your teammates and coaches while rehabilitating?

Other thoughts:

Additional Journal Prompts

1. *The Natural*

If you're a natural athlete, describe what it's like to someone who is not. If you're not a natural athlete, write about what it's like to train with or compete against someone who is. If you are a natural athlete, what's your biggest frustration. If you are not a natural athlete, why has that been a good thing for you?

2. *Failure*

Professor Dan Gerdes asked his sports psychology students to explore how failure can be helpful. Among the list his students compiled were the following—write about them:

> *Failure found what didn't work.*
> *Failure creates hunger to do better.*
> *Failure adds value to success.*
> *Failure is feedback.*

3. Tell about a time when you were genuinely happy for another athlete's poor performance or loss.

4. Describe your greatest disappointment as an athlete thus far in your career. What did you learn from the experience?

5. Who's the oldest athlete you know. Describe the athlete. What characteristics of the athlete do you admire?

6. Describe your earliest memory as an athlete.

7. If you could relive one moment as an athlete, what would it be and why would you want to go back?

8. "Champions aren't made in the gyms. Champions are made from something they have deep inside them ~ a desire, a dream, a vision."

> – Muhammad Ali

Write about this quotation from the great heavy weight boxer Muhammad Ali.

9. *Tell about a time when you quit.*

10. Have you ever been dishonest as an athlete? If so, why? What did you learn from this experience? If you haven't been dishonest or don't want to write about it, have you witnessed dishonesty on the part of another athlete? If so, how did it make you feel?

11. At the present moment what three non-athletic jobs look as if they might give you the same "feeling" that competitive athletics do? Explain you thinking.

12. Where do you see yourself in the next few years as an athlete?

13. What is something you dislike about yourself as an athlete?
14. Think back to a time when an athlete you knew or admired bombed big-time in an event that he or she was favored to win. Describe your feelings.

15. What is your favorite place to compete and why?

16. Write about a frustrating experience you've had as an athlete.

17. When is training an absolute joy?

18. Under what circumstances would you allow a competitor to beat you on purpose.

19 What books would you recommend to a young athlete?

20. Your coach or assistant coach gave you misinformation before big competition.

21. Write from the perspective of the top athlete in your sport using any of these prompts—

> "When I win a competition by a wide margin, I..."
> "My worst performance in the past six months made me feel..."
> "When other athletes talk about me they say..."
> "I am frightened about..."

22. Tape your favorite newspaper article about your season in the Notes section of this workbook. If you or your team didn't make the newspapers, print and include a favorite Facebook or blog post. Write about what has been written.

23. Write about the following quotation by alpine ski racer Carter Robinson: "No one likes skiing with a cluttered mind, so put it on paper and free some space."

24. Create a crossword puzzle of your sport or team with a free online program like http://www.puzzle-maker.com/CW/

25. Found Poem: Honest... the following activity is fun and helps athletes see a game more clearly by thinking more deeply. Here are the steps toward creating a Found Poem:

- Find a newspaper article written about you, your team, or another athlete/team that you admire;

- Read the article and underline words, phrases, or lines that you like or find interesting. Put those words, phrases, or lines into a non-rhyming poem that tells a story. Here are a few paragraphs from an article by Kalle Oakes in today's newspaper (*Sun Journal*, 11/14/2010) about our hometown football team's victory in the regional playoff championship. I've underlined some favorite words and phrases that I might use in a poem. I've also added a few of my own words to a Found Poem I began:

> **Falcons** Squelch **Warriors**, Win **Eighth** Regional Title
>
> RUMFORD — Mountain Valley High School has boasted bigger football teams. More **explosive** football teams. Teams with more players whose names roll off the tongue in hushed, reverential tones.
>
> Tough to think of one, offhand, that has played better defense.
>
> The **undefeated**, rarely challenged Falcons allowed only five first downs and 87 net yards Saturday in an 18-0 **whitewashing** of Wells in the Western Class B championship at Chet Bulger Field.

> Here's the opening to a Found Poem:
>
> EIGHT
>
> Undefeated
>
> And rarely challenged—
>
> Our explosive Falcons
>
> Whitewashed Wells
>
> For number eight....

26. If I were not competing in my sport, I would be _____ because _____.

Then... explain your thinking.

27. *What was I thinking?* Go back through your journal and log and pick out the comical, nonsensical, and mindless lines you've written and write them below. Enjoy...

28. Watch a competition on television or online and make a list of the best lines spoken by the commentators, coaches, or athletes.

29. Note to an Opponent: After a game or competition, write a note to an opponent. You might write to the primary person you defended or played against. If your sport is like baseball or track, pick an opponent who performed exceptionally well or who struggled. Highlight an opponent's strengths or weaknesses. In the case of an opponent's weakness, offer some advice. Here's an example from a high school soccer match:

> *Dear # 3 Right Back,*
>
> *We played against each other on Thursday night and* <u>*you could not stop me*</u>*. Every time I attacked with the ball down the left touchline you lunged at the ball–you ALWAYS tried to take the ball away from me and never really just tried to delay my attack. My coach tells us that there are four D's in defending–*
>
> > *-Deny the opponent the ball*
> > *-Delay the opponent when he has the ball*
> > *-Destroy... win the ball!]*
> > *-Develop an attack once you have ball*
>
> *You should practice shadowing an attacking offender, pushing him to the touchline so he can't get a full look at the goal. Delaying stops him from advancing toward the goal and gets other players behind the ball to defend. When the player miskicks the ball or plays it too far ahead, you win the ball. I'm glad I'm not really giving you this letter because I like playing against you! I scored and got two assists. HA! See you in a few weeks, sucka.*
>
> *Your nightmare,*
> *Chad*
> *Sailors #9*

27. Video Comments: If you or your team had a video taken of a game, match, race, or performance, write a paragraph summarizing the competition as if you were the team's public relations person or a sports caster summarizing the game for television.

28. If appropriate, trade workbooks with a teammate or friend and write an observation of the athlete with respect to training, competition, or life beyond athletics.

29. Draw a picture of a particular moment from the season.

30. As someone who is keeping a journal, how do you feel about this quotation by Grace Paley: "We write about what we don't know about what we know."

31. Write about this quotation from Boston Marathon winner Amby Burfoot: "To get to the finish line, you'll have to try lots of different paths."

32. Write a caption for this a fun photo:

Caption: _____

33. Pre-game or pre-competition study: answer the following about the opponent you are about to face:

> If you have played this opponent before, what do you remember about the last contest?
> What have reliable sources said about the opponents' strengths and weaknesses?

What's one strategy or approach that you or your team should try against this opponent?

What's your overall game plan?

34. Write about this quotation from basketball legend Michael Jordan: "I've missed more than 9000 shots in my career. I've lost almost 300 games. 26 times, I've been trusted to take the game winning shot and missed. I've failed over and over and over again in my life. And that is why I succeed."

35. Dr. Stephanie Dowrick identifies the following benefits of journaling:
-   reduce stress and anxiety
-   increase self-awareness
-   sharpen mental skills
-   promote genuine psychological insight
-   advance creative inspiration and insight
-   strengthen coping abilities

Have you experienced any of these benefits?

36. After a competition you participated in, write a performance analysis of a teammate or fellow athlete.

37. Write some six-word sports stories about your competitions and training. Here's an example from a hockey playoff game: "Into OT— Hail Mary empty netter." Or one on training: "Yearlong training; offseason camps: Made Varsity."

38. All professional teams and some collegiate teams have the support of sport psychologists. Their work involves helping athletes with a wide range of issues such as
-   Mental preparedness
-   Managing Anxiety
-   Coping with Success
-   Handling Failure
-   Goal setting
-   Reward strategies
-   Visualization
-   Motivation

Has writing in this workbook helped you with any of these concerns. If you're not familiar with some of these issues, just do a quick search online.

39. One writing scholar wrote the following:

"Writing organizes and clarifies our thoughts. Writing is how we think our way into a subject and make it our own. Writing enables us to find out what we know—and what we don't know—about whatever we're trying to learn." –William Zinsser, *Writing to Learn*

In what ways is this quotation true for you as an athlete who writes?

40. Why can taking a day off be difficult for you?

41. Look back at the results of the last competition you won or did well in. Think about the losing team or look at the name and time of the last-place finisher. Write from the perspective of a player on the losing team or the last-place finisher.

42. Write a conversation between you and an incredibly gifted young athlete who is not living up to her or his potential.

43. Write about the following quotation by Alberto Tomba, an Italian Ski Racer: "In life, I have but one simple desire: To tear down the sky."

44. Describe what it's like to hit "the wall" during training or a competition.

45. Describe an athlete you would never want to be a teammate with.

46. *Flip it.* If you're an athlete not participating on a team (e.g., a road runner), write about what it would be like to be on a team. If you're on a team (e.g., water polo), write about what it would be like to be an individual athlete.

47. What's the best competition you've ever seen in person as a fan?

48. Remember and write about the biggest disappointment you've experienced as an athlete.

49. Truth is, this season...

50. Describe your experience writing in this workbook and send your thoughts to me: Rich Kent (rich.kent@maine.edu).

Notes Pages

NOTES_____   DATE_____

NOTES_____   DATE_____

NOTES_____ DATE_____

_____

_____

_____

_____

_____

_____

_____

_____

NOTES_____   DATE_____

NOTES_____   DATE_____

NOTES_____   DATE_____

NOTES_____   DATE_____

NOTES_____   DATE_____

NOTES_____   DATE_____

NOTES_____   DATE_____

NOTES_____   DATE_____

NOTES_____   DATE_____

NOTES_____   DATE_____

NOTES_____   DATE_____

NOTES_____   DATE_____

NOTES_____   DATE_____

NOTES_____   DATE_____

NOTES_____   DATE_____

NOTES_____   DATE_____

NOTES_____ DATE_____

Write. Learn. Perform.
Keep training.

Made in the USA
San Bernardino, CA
28 November 2019